Igor Ostapenko is an engineer by education, specializing in corporate training and development within the oil and gas industry. Since 2006, he has been actively involved in teaching, managing instructional teams, and organizing engineering classes. Igor also takes a leadership role in coordinating English language and soft skills training, while designing comprehensive training programs. With his extensive expertise and unwavering commitment, Igor has made substantial contributions that greatly impacted the growth and success of multiple organizations in the industry. His passion for education and continuous improvement remains the driving force behind his impactful work in corporate training and development.

Igor Ostapenko

ALL ENGLISH TENSES IN ONE SIMPLE CHART

AUSTIN MACAULEY PUBLISHERS™
LONDON * CAMBRIDGE * NEW YORK * SHARJAH

Ordering Information
Quantity sales: Special discounts are available on quantity purchases by corporations, associations, and others. For details, contact the publisher at the address below.

Publisher's Cataloging-in-Publication data
Ostapenko, Igor
All English Tenses in One Simple Chart

ISBN 9798889108849 (Paperback)
ISBN 9798889108856 (ePub e-book)

Library of Congress Control Number: 2023924611

www.austinmacauley.com/us

First Published 2024
Austin Macauley Publishers LLC
40 Wall Street, 33rd Floor, Suite 3302
New York, NY 10005
USA

mail-usa@austinmacauley.com
+1 (646) 5125767

Thanks to all my friends and students, who served as patient guinea pigs in the testing of this teaching method, this book is dedicated. Your unwavering support and invaluable feedback have shaped its pages, and I am deeply grateful for your enduring commitment to learning and growth.

Table of Contents

English Tenses 9

About This Course 10

The Short Answer to the Question: Why Does English Have So Many Tenses? 11

How to Read the Diagrams in This Book 22

Question No 1 How Many Tenses Does English Have? 41

Question No 2 What Types of Verbs Does English Have? 68

Question No 3 What Are the Verb Forms? 72

Let's Start Studying the Chart for the Main 12 Tenses (Active Voice) 100

The Main Chart! 122

Asking a Question 147

The 'Extra' Auxiliary Verb 155

So! How Do We Form a Question? 160

How Do You Form a Negative? 163

Using English Tenses 166

Speaking About the Past 168

Speaking About the Future 173

English Tenses — Frequency of Use 176

Passive Voice 178

Question — Through a Question Word 188

Reported (Indirect) Speech   191

Future in the Past   202

Grammatical Forms   207

Conditionals   212

Practice Exercise   221

Let's Close a Couple of Very Common Gaps: 239

What to Do Now?   242

English Tenses

— How many are there?

— My God! Why so many?

— Do they actually use them all?

— How do I form a damn sentence?

— How do I ask a question?

— And how in the world am I supposed to memorize all this?

About This Course

For many English-language learners, tenses are the most difficult topic because they do not understand them. Feeling frustrated and stuck, they never make significant progress.

But learning a language — under the right conditions — should be fun. Using English tenses properly becomes simple with the 'hack' I share in this course.

So, let's cross this mighty river once and for all, so you can start enjoying your language acquisition journey.

In a couple of hours, you will be easily navigating active and passive voice tenses. You will be forming questions and negative sentences in any tense.

How Does This Course Work?

Different cultures have different ways of memorizing stuff. In Russia, if you want to remember how to tighten a bolt, you'll probably look at your right hand (your slightly bent fingers show how to turn the bolt, and your thumb shows the direction a bolt moves). In the United States, you might use the mnemonic *'righty tighty, lefty loosy'* (turn right to tighten — turn left to loosen).

And you probably won't remember the order of the colors of the rainbow without the mnemonic, *'Richard Of York Gave Battle In Vain'*, or the equivalent in your language. In Russian, it's *'Каждый охотник желает знать, где сидит фазан'*. The first letter of each word corresponds to a specific color…red, orange, yellow, green, blue, indigo, and violet.

The method I present here helps with English tenses in much the same way. It will help you remember very easily.

The Short Answer to the Question: Why Does English Have So Many Tenses?

- Tenses convey shades of meaning; they specify and accentuate things. They add nuances.
- In English, it's easy to give a lot of information in a short sentence — much easier than in Russian, for example. Fun fact: one page of English text turns into 1.5 pages of Russian translation because you need more Russian words to convey the same amount of information.
- Don't believe English language teachers who claim that you can get by using three or four tenses and that the rest are useless. Do not make your English stiff by limiting your grammatical range.

Why aren't we speaking English properly? What's wrong with our school courses?

The short answer to this question is:
This is a complex problem!
The education system is awkward and completely outdated.

Most non-native ESL teachers do not know English well.

- They can follow the textbook along with the students, but even a minor digression from it would completely confuse them.
- Unfortunately, non-native ESL teachers are not paid well. They do not travel the world, getting much language practice themselves.
- A certificate from a cheesy two-week course at a random language school in Malta is often all you can expect them to have. And you can

forget about finding a teacher of Business English who knows anything about business!

In schools, the standard approach is to follow the textbook or teaching manual.

In Russia, they still print old textbooks with outdated Briticisms:

Examples: *you have not* (instead of: *you don't have*), *she has got* (instead of: *she has*), *I shall do* (instead of: *I will do*)

Here is a quote from the Russian writer Mikhail Veller.
It's about learning French, but the point is the same.

*"He was secretly seeing a French teacher; his wife felt that something's going on and was jealous, even though the teacher was old and ugly. The teacher was happy to find a kindred spirit; **she also never visited Paris, and was taught French in a university by professors who also never visited Paris, using textbooks written by people who never visited it either.**"*

— Mikhail Veller, "I want to go to Paris"

Having a native speaker as a teacher is not the solution. At the beginning of your journey, it may even be counter-productive.

The Goal of This Course...

...is to teach you all there is to know about English tenses, show you how they relate to one another, and let you in on the best-kept secret that...

...English tenses are actually super-easy!

When you're learning English tenses, you need to look at them in connection to each other.

Don't study them separately.

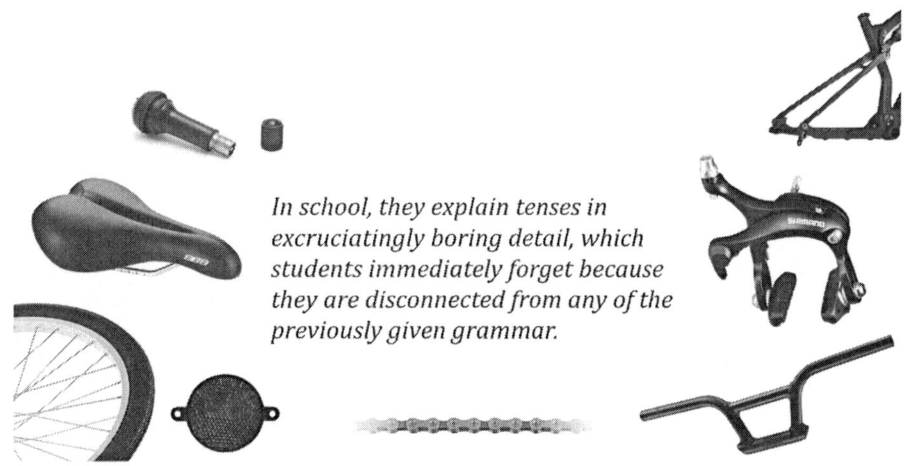

In school, they explain tenses in excruciatingly boring detail, which students immediately forget because they are disconnected from any of the previously given grammar.

Students are left to connect the pieces on their own. God knows how they will manage that!

There's a mathematical beauty to English tenses.

When you learn them, you will need to memorize less information than the multiplication table.

In this course, you will memorize how English tenses are formed in the same way that *'Richard Of York Gave Battle In Vain',* helps you remember the colors of the rainbow.

Once you learn the mnemonic formula, you will never confuse the tenses again.

Do not overload yourself with grammar rules. Try to understand how they work.

"What you understand, you know; and what you know, you don't forget!"

— Michel Thomas, polyglot, author of 'The Michel Thomas Method'

You just need to understand how this chart works:

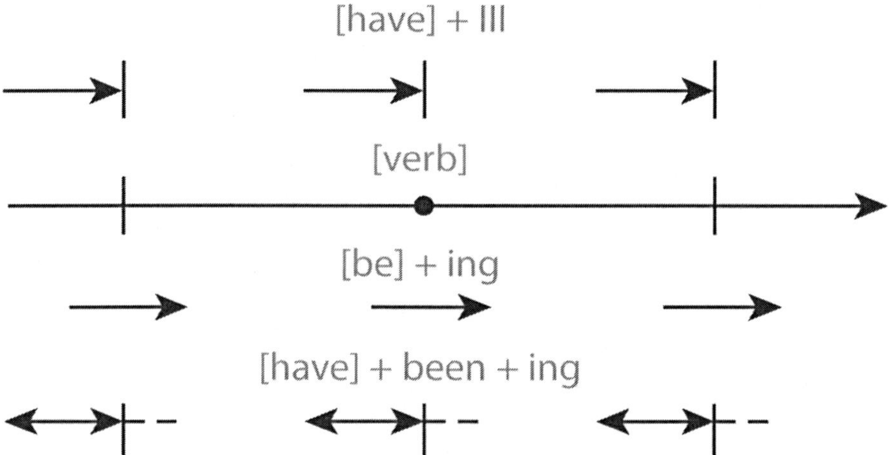

But before we get to the chart, I need to explain a few things.

How to Read the Diagrams in This Book

Past ← Present → Future

We'll be using arrows to show how a verb changes across Present, Past, and Future tenses.

did ← do → will do
had ← have → will have
took ← take → will take

We'll be using square brackets sometimes to show the base form of a changing verb.

[be] — possible forms: *am, is, are*
[do] — possible forms: *do, does*
[have] — possible forms: *have* or *has*
[verb] — any action verb in its base form
(+ *–s* or *–es* for the third-person singular)

An important rule: Get rid of all the extra stuff.

While you are still practicing, use this little rule:

If a sentence confuses you, get rid of all the extra stuff. Just leave the subject and the predicate (*who does what*) — this way, you can focus on understanding how tenses work. After you finish analyzing your sentence, put everything back.

Here are a few examples:

The grandmother is making ~~a cake for the children~~
I saw ~~him by chance in the tram two days ago~~
He ~~sometimes~~ drinks ~~coffee in the morning~~

The following things are super-basic for most students, but let's make sure everyone understands them before we go further.

So, here is a quick refresher:

Word Order

does something (verb)

subject + predicate + object

someone (or something)   to something (or someone) else

Word order (in more detail)

subject	predicate	object		
		indirect object (no preposition)	direct	indirect object (with preposition)
Lisa	*gave*	*me*	*a book*	*to me*
I	*read*		*a book*	

adverbial modifier		
...of place	...of time	...of manner
	two years ago	
in this room	*every day*	*with great interest*

less often   more often

's can mean different things

Lisa's — **possessive case**
Example: *This is Lisa's cat.* (This cat belongs to Lisa.)

Lisa's — **contraction of "Lisa is"**
Example: *Lisa's a great musician.* (Lisa is a great musician.)

Lisa's — **contraction of "Lisa has"**
Example*: Lisa's never been late.* (Lisa has never been late.)

Do not confuse *it's* and *its*

it's

1.   The contraction of *'it is'*.

Example: *The city's population is over a million. It's [it is] huge.*

2.   The contraction of *'it has'*.

Example: *It's been [it has been] so long since we last saw each other.*

its

The **possessive pronoun *its***.

Example: *The city is huge. Its population is more than a million.*

Very Common Contractions

- I am — I'm
- I will — I'll
- I have — I've
- I had — I'd (less often)
- I would — I'd (more often)
- he is — he's
- he has — he's
- she is — she's
- she has — she's
- it is — it's
- it has — it's
- we are — we're
- do not — don't
- did not — didn't
- was not — wasn't
- were not — weren't
- have not — haven't
- had not — hadn't
- cannot — can't
- will not — won't

Other Common Contractions

- must not — mustn't
- should not — shouldn't
- what is — what's
- where is — where's
- how is — how's

These contractions are used in informal spoken English a lot!

- going to — gonna
- want to — wanna
- got to — gotta

— I'm gonna go.
— I wanna go home.
— I gotta go!

In spoken and informal written English, contractions are used almost exclusively except when you want to add emphasis by using the full form.

— *I don't smoke.* (I don't have the habit of smoking.)
— *I do not smoke.* (I REALLY do not have this habit!)

Other ways of emphasizing an idea:

1. **Inversion** (the reversal of the normal word order):
    Never have I seen such beauty! (more emphasis)
    Instead of: *I have never seen such beauty.* (less emphasis)

2. **Exaggerated pronunciation**: The pronunciation of the indefinite article 'a' as [eɪ] instead of [ə].

    It is a great deal! (Fun fact: Donald Trump used this trick a lot in his speeches.)
    Or the pronunciation of the definite article "the" as [ðiː] instead of [ðə].

Another way to emphasize something is by adding an extra [do] before the main verb.

We'll be using this method a lot in this course. It helps with questions and negative forms of sentences in the Present Simple and Past Simple (details later).
   — *I know how to type.* (I have this skill.)
   — *I do know how to type!* (I REALLY have this skill!)

Make sure you know how to form the third-person singular!

The grammar rule is very simple:
To form the third-person singular (*he, she, it*) in the Present, you add an extra *–s* or *–es* to the end of the verb.

For example: *I go — he goes; we do — she does; they shine — it shines.*

The verb *have* turns into *has* — *he has, she has, it has.* (Notice that it also ends in *–s.*)

The ending *–s* disappears in the Past and Future tenses.

he had ← he has → he will have
he went ← he goes → he will go

Compare it to the first-person singular (pronoun: *I*):

I had ← I have → I will have
I went ← I go → I will go

–es

Add an –es, if a verb ends in: –s, –ss, –zz, –sh, –ch, –x, –o
I wish → he wishes
you go → she goes
we fix → it fixes

When a verb ends in a consonant, you add –y:
then –y turns to –i
and you add –es

I carry → he carries

–s

In all other cases, simply add *–s*

I read → he reads
you sing → she sings
we sleep → it sleeps

The Third-Person Singular + Modal Verbs

A quick review: To form the third-person singular (*he, she, it*) in the Present tense, verbs get an extra letter *–s* or *–es* at the end.

But if there's a modal verb (*can, may, must*) in front of the main verb, it steals the *–s* ending from the main verb but does not change itself.

An exception to the rule is the modal verb *have to*. For the third-person singular, it will turn into *has to*.

She swims — she can swim
She goes — she has to go

Be, Do, Have

Make sure you know how these common modal verbs change in the Past and Future tenses.

To Be (Linking Verb)

Formula: was (were) ← [be] → will be

In the Future, it's always *will be.*
In the Past, it's was in the singular and were in the plural.

- *I was ← I am → I will be*
- *he was ← he is → he will be*
- *she was ← she is → she will be*
- *it was ← it is → it will be*
- *we were ← we are → we will be*
- *they were ← they are → they will be*
- *you were ← you are → you will be*

! In Modern English, *YOU* is the second-person pronoun. Although it is grammatically plural, it is used for all cases and numbers (singular *you* — one person; plural *you* — a group of people). This is why '*you ARE*' (singular) is the same as '*we ARE*' and '*they ARE*' (plural).

To do

Formula: did ← [do] → will do

Past (always) — *did*, Future (always) — *will do*

- *I did ← I do → I will do*
- *you did ← you do → you will do*
- *he did ← he does → he will do*
- *she did ← she does → she will do*
- *it did ← it does → it will do*
- *we did ← we do → we will do*
- *they did ← they do → they will do*

To have

Formula: had ← [have] → will have
Don't forget: in the Present, *have* becomes *has* for *he, she, it*.

Past (always) — *had*, Future (always) — *will have*

- *I had ← I have → I will have*
- *you had ← you have → you will have*
- *he had ← he has → he will have*
- *she had ← she has → she will have*
- *it had ← it has → it will have*
- *we had ← we have → we will have*
- *they had ← they have → they will have*

Shall

- *Shall* is an obsolete way of talking about the future. Use *will* instead. But you may come across *shall* in old or stylized texts and legal documents.
- You'll understand when and how to use *shall* as you progress in your ESL journey, but for now, it's enough to say that it is mostly used in invitations to start something, like a meeting or meal. For example, *Shall we eat?*
- Another use is for when you find yourself in a similar pickle as Gandalf in *'The Lord of the Rings'*.

Let's answer these three questions:

1. How many tenses does English have?
2. What types of verbs does it have?
3. What are its verb forms?

Question No 1
How Many Tenses Does English Have?

The short answer: **Linguists cannot agree on that, still!**

If you've been struggling with English for a long time, you've probably heard different answers to this question.

While there is some agreement, certain things are still debated.

Some linguists argue that there are only three tenses (Present, Past, and Future) and that the rest are *aspects, structures,* and *formulas*. In part, they are right.

But let's leave such discussions to the professionals. My guess is that you are not writing a dissertation on linguistics at the moment.

More or less, the answer is:

- **Active Voice (12 tenses)**
- **Passive Voice (8 tenses)**
- Future in the Past (4 tenses)
- Future in the Past – Passive Voice (2 tenses)
- Other (grammatical) forms:
— going to
— used to

In Active Voice, the grammatical subject performs or causes the action denoted by the verb *(he/she/it does something)*.

— *I opened the door*

Passive Voice

In Passive Voice, the grammatical subject is the recipient of the action denoted by the verb *(someone does something to him/her/it.).*

— *The door was opened* *(by him)*

Sometimes we specify the Agent of the action
(the one who is causing it),
and sometimes we omit them

So, how does the chart work?

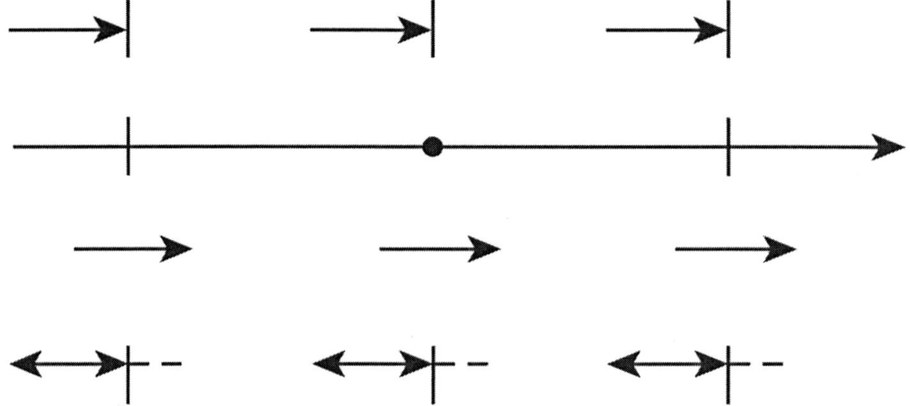

Three 'columns' for the Tenses — four 'lines' for the Aspects

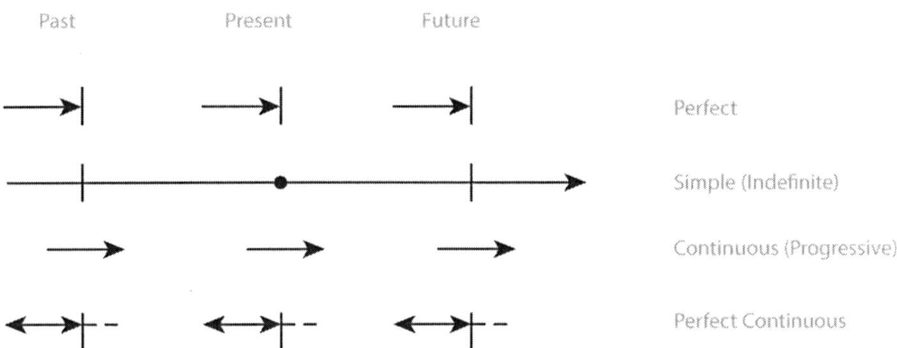

Please note that in different books you may encounter different names for the tenses!

- Simple = Indefinite
- Continuous = Progressive

Past

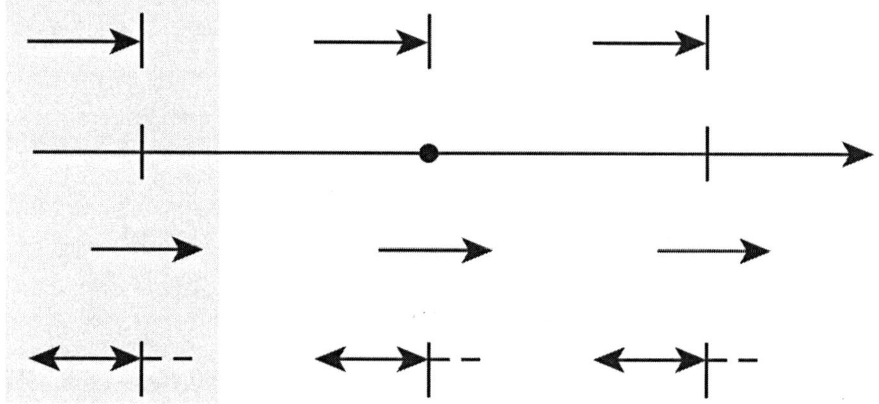

Present

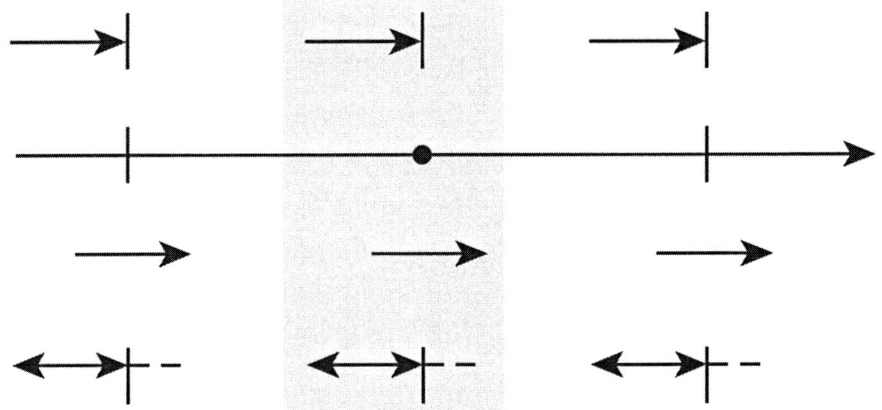

Future

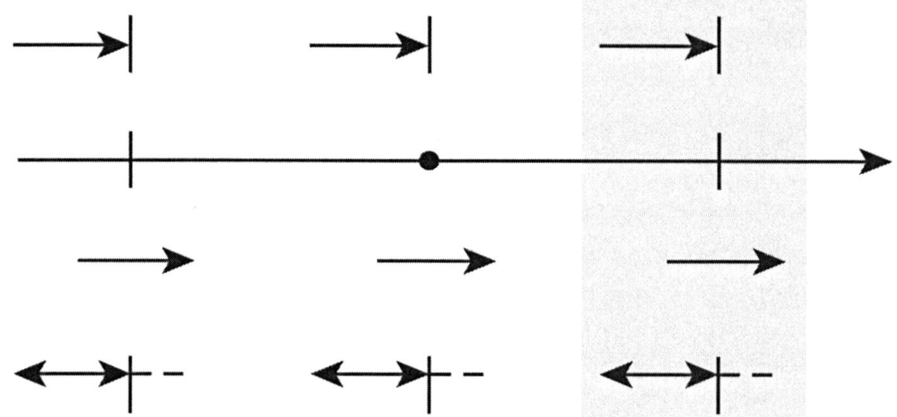

Perfect

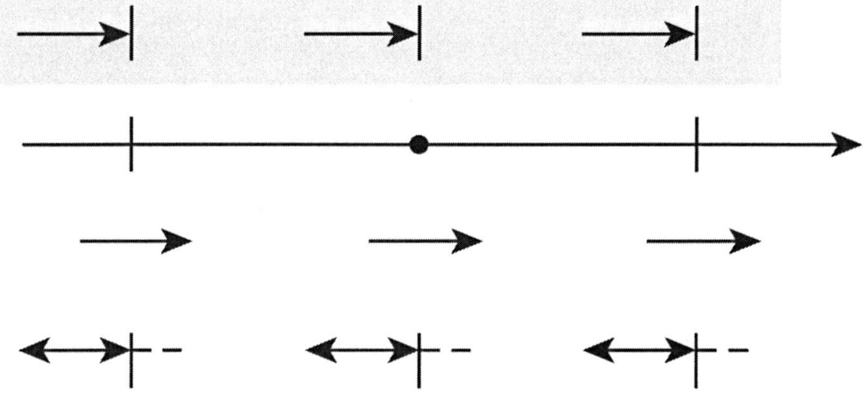

Simple (Indefinite)

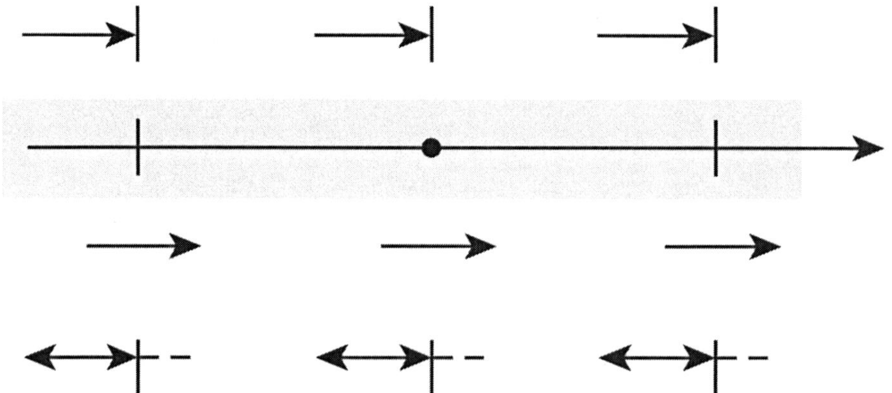

Continuous (Progressive)

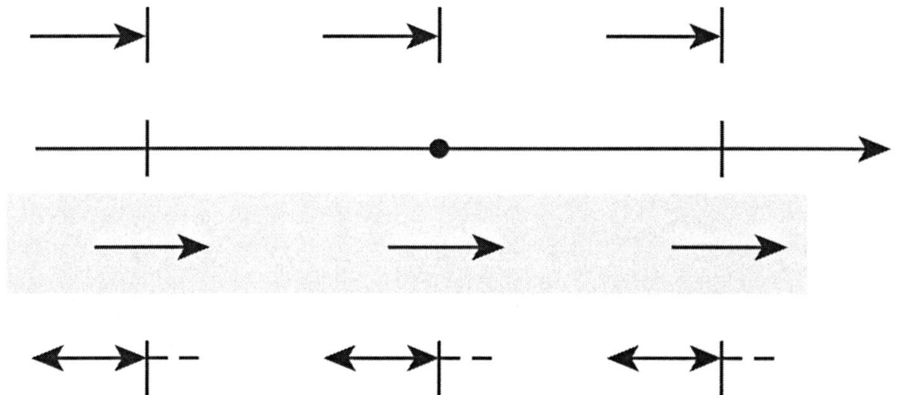

Perfect-Continuous

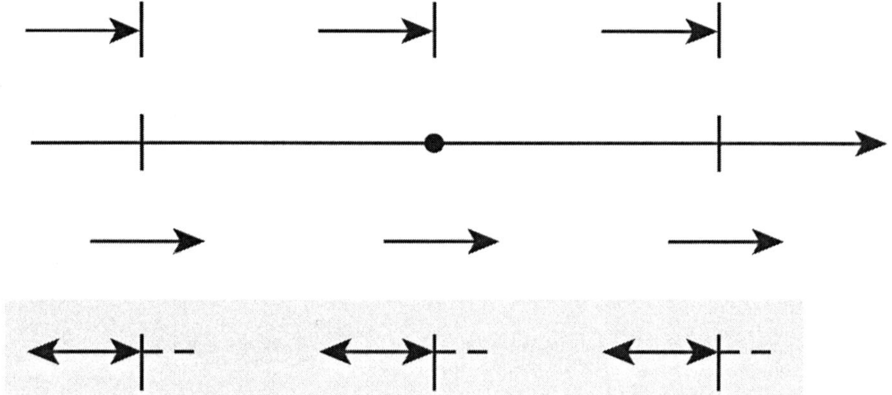

Now — The intersections...

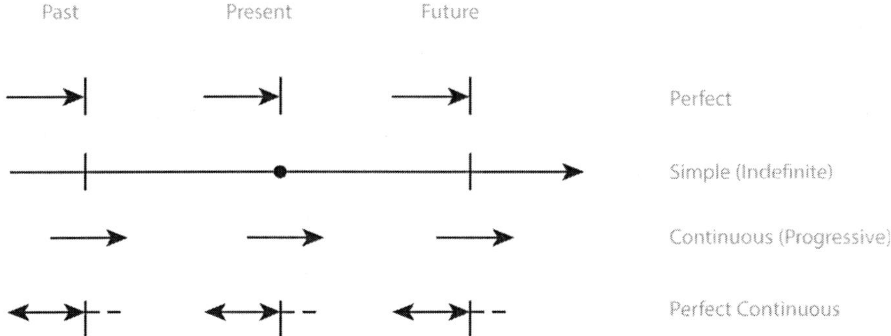

Present Perfect

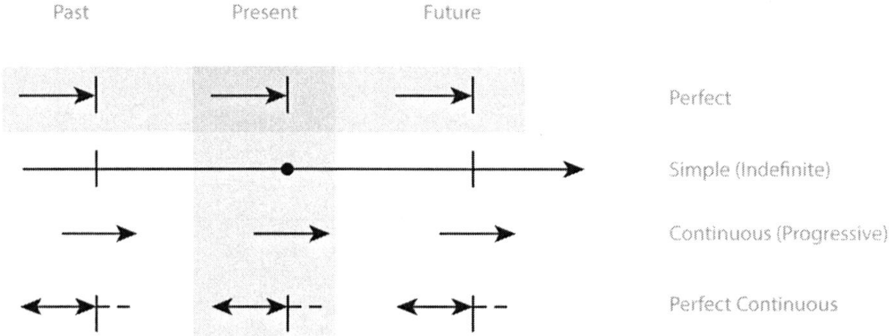

Present Simple

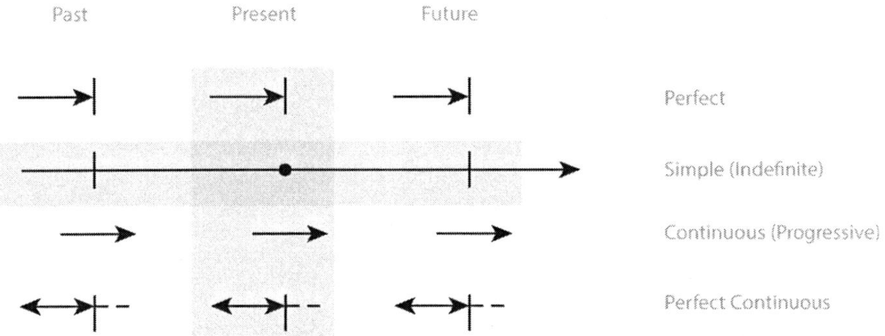

Present Continuous

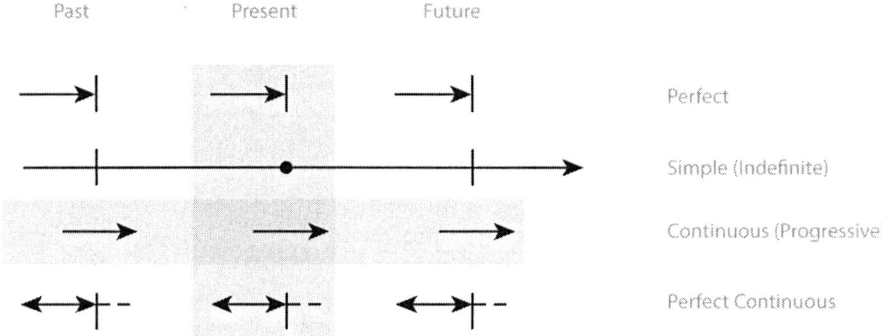

Present Perfect-Continuous

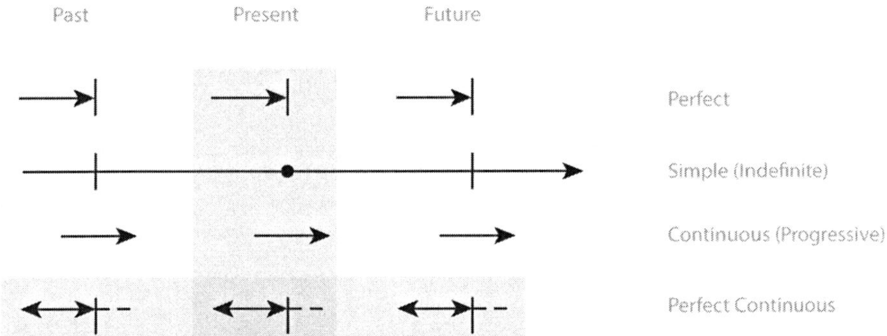

Future Perfect

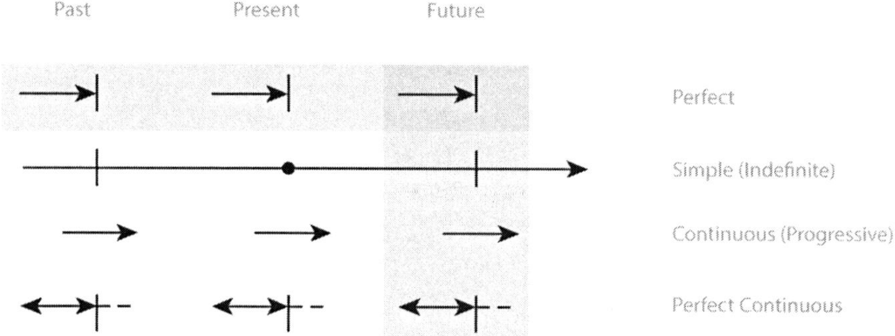

Future Simple

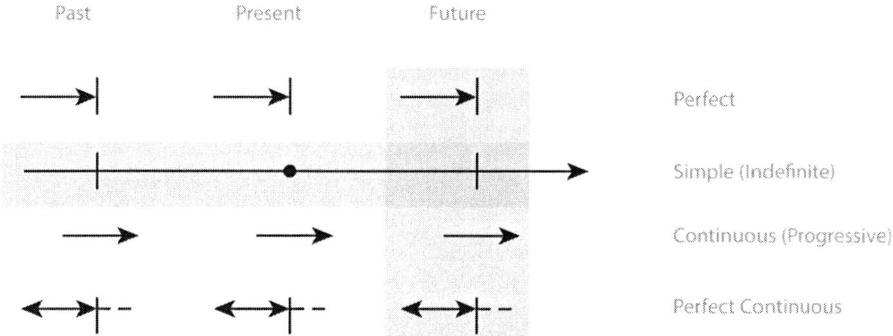

Future Continuous

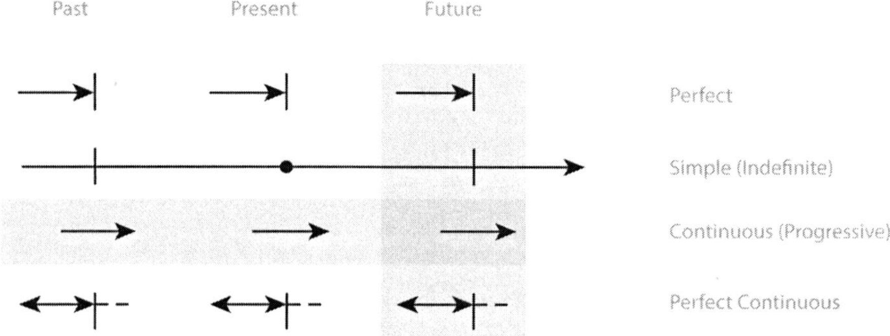

Future Perfect-Continuous

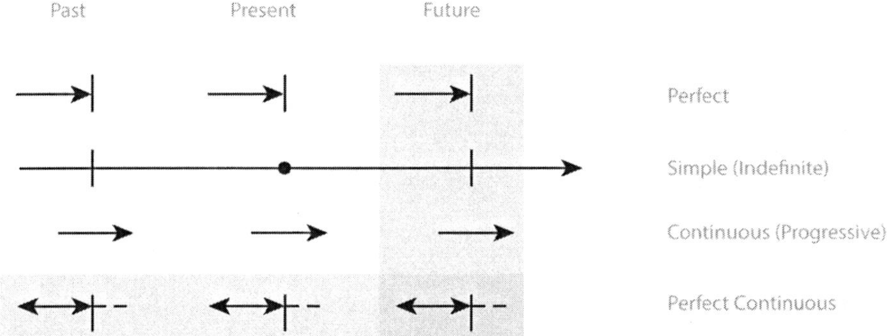

Past Perfect

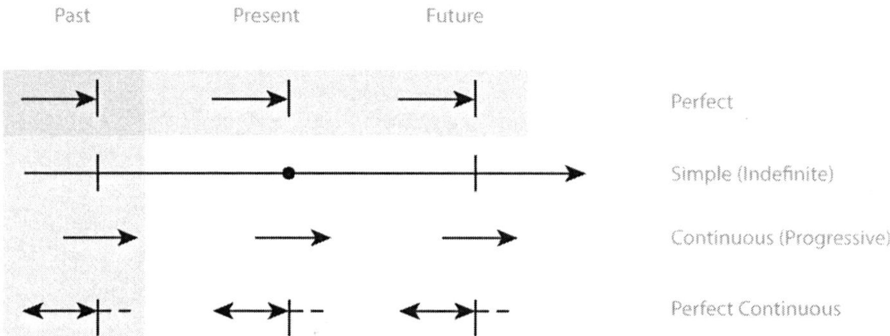

Past Simple

Past
Present
Future
Perfect
Simple (Indefinite)
Continuous (Progressive)
Perfect Continuous

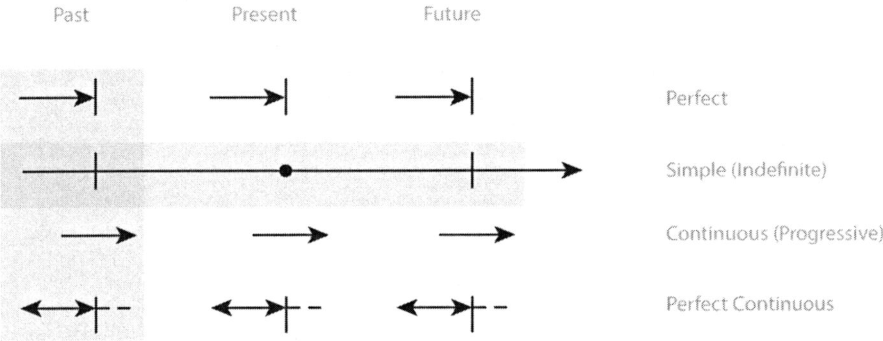

Past Continuous

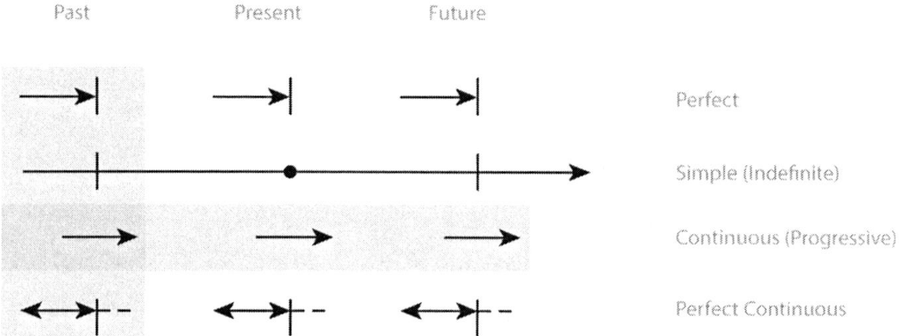

Past Perfect Continuous

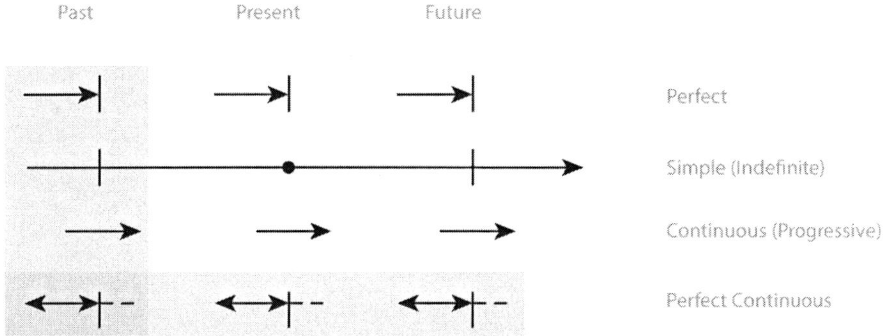

So, how many tenses? 3×4=12

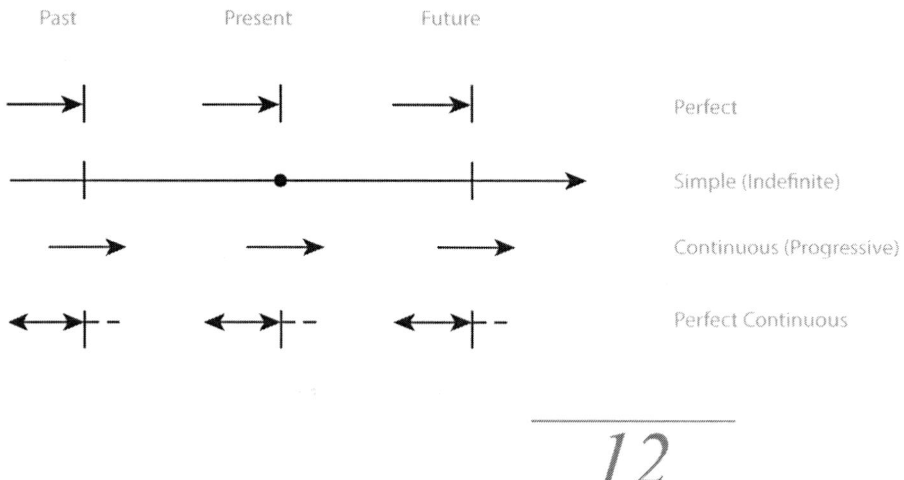

12

Twelve main tenses (Active Voice)

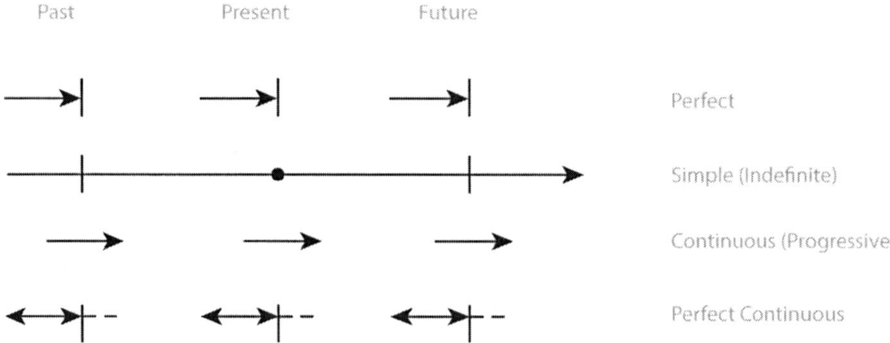

We're running ahead of ourselves, but for the Passive Voice this is how the chart will look:

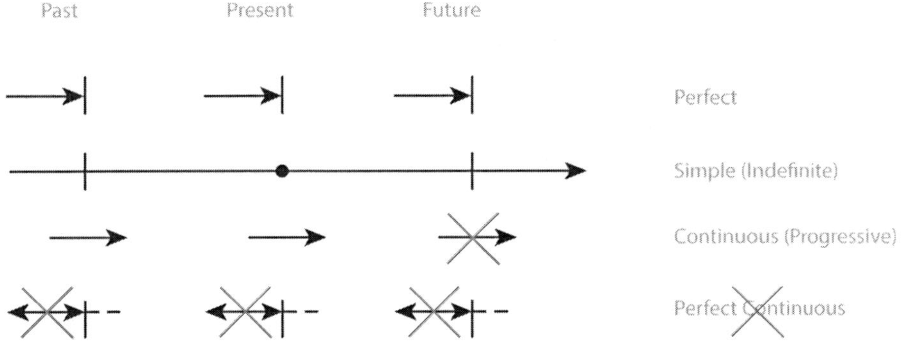

8 more tenses!

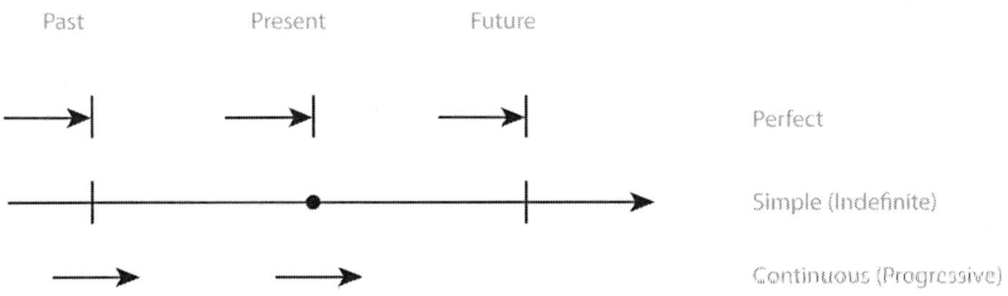

So!

12 — Tenses in Active Voice

8 — Tenses in Passive Voice

Question No 2
What Types of Verbs Does English Have?

There are many classifications, but we are talking about functions:

- **Main (Action)** verbs
- **Helping** or **Auxiliary verbs** (Primary Auxiliary Verbs, Linking Verbs, Modal Verbs)

Main (Action) Verbs

I have *done*

main verb

Auxiliary Verbs

I have done

auxiliary verb

Three auxiliary verbs you absolutely need to master:

be, do, have

Linking Verbs

Linking verbs are not followed by objects. Instead, they are followed by phrases that give extra information about the subject (e.g., noun phrases, adjective phrases, adverb phrases, or prepositional phrases).

Examples: *be, become, come, grow, turn, appear, seem, keep, remain, stay, look, sound, feel, taste, smell.*

!   Different sources use different names, such as:
linking verbs, copulative verbs, state-of-being verbs, or *being verbs*

Modal Verbs

Modal verbs have meanings connected with degrees of certainty and necessity.
So, they only can be used together with a main verb.

I can swim.
You have to go.

Examples of modal verbs: *can (could); may (might); must; have to (have got to); be to; need; ought to; should; would; shall; will; dare; used to.*

Main (Action) verbs
&
Helping or Auxiliary verbs

- *Primary Auxiliary*
- *Linking*
- *Modal*

Question No 3
What Are the Verb Forms?

In school, we memorize three forms of irregular verbs. The problem is, not everyone understands what they are memorizing.

Three verb forms:

$$\textit{open} \rightarrow \textit{opened} \rightarrow \textit{opened}$$

I (V1) — Base Form

$$open \rightarrow opened \rightarrow opened$$

! The base form of the verb is identical to the dictionary entry; it does not bear any agreement, tense, or participle ending.

II (V2) — Past Tense

open → opened → opened

We use the Simple Past tense to express an action completed at a specific time in the past — it was performed only once and completed in the past. *I opened a bottle.*

III (V3) — Past Participle

$$open \rightarrow opened \rightarrow opened$$

It bears some qualities of an adjective — a word that describes a noun or a pronoun.

!

1) *I have opened* (a window)
2) *the window was opened*
3) *an opened bottle*

Verb Conjugation

There are two types of verbs when it comes to their conjugations:

- Regular
- Irregular

Regular

Regular verbs form their past and past participle forms by adding *–ed.*

$$open \rightarrow opened \rightarrow opened$$

Irregular

Irregular verbs form their Past and Past Participle forms in different ways — this means that the rule of simply adding *–ed* does not apply to them.

There are mainly three types of irregular verbs.
- Verbs in which all three forms are the same (e.g. *put — put — put*).
- Verbs in which two of the three forms are the same (e.g. *sit — sat — sat*).
- Verbs in which all three forms are different (e.g. *drink — drank — drunk*).

So, you're gonna have to learn them!

There are more than 200* irregular verbs, but only 50 are common.

My advice: Start by learning the 50 common verbs.
You can look up the others in a dictionary.
But without those 50, you will always be lost.

! * — In fact, there are 638 irregular verbs, but most are so rare and obsolete that we can easily disregard them.

The table cells containing similar-looking forms are highlighted in gray.

Infinitive	Past Simple	Past Participle
be	was / were	been
become	became	become
begin	began	begun
bring	brought	brought
buy	bought	bought
choose	chose	chosen
come	came	come
do	did	done
drink	drank	drunk
drive	drove	driven
eat	ate	eaten
fall	fell	fallen

Infinitive	Past Simple	Past Participle
feel	felt	felt
find	found	found
fly	flew	flown
forget	forgot	forgotten
get	got	got (US: gotten)
give	gave	given
go	went	gone
have	had	had
hear	heard	heard
keep	kept	kept
know	knew	known
leave	left	left
lend	lent	lent

Infinitive	Past Simple	Past Participle
let	let	let
lose	lost	lost
make	made	made
meet	met	met
pay	paid	paid
put	put	put
read	read ("red")	read ("red")
run	ran	run
say	said	said
see	saw	seen
sell	sold	sold
send	sent	sent

Infinitive	Past Simple	Past Participle
sing	sang	sung
sit	sat	sat
sleep	slept	slept
speak	spoke	spoken
stand	stood	stood
swim	swam	swum
take	took	taken
teach	taught	taught
tell	told	told
think	thought	thought
understand	understood	understood
wear	wore	worn
write	wrote	written

II form — 'Past Tense' (Past Form)

Despite its name, the II verb form (V2, Past Form) is only used to form the Past Simple and only for affirmative sentences (+) — not for questions and negative sentences.

That means only here:

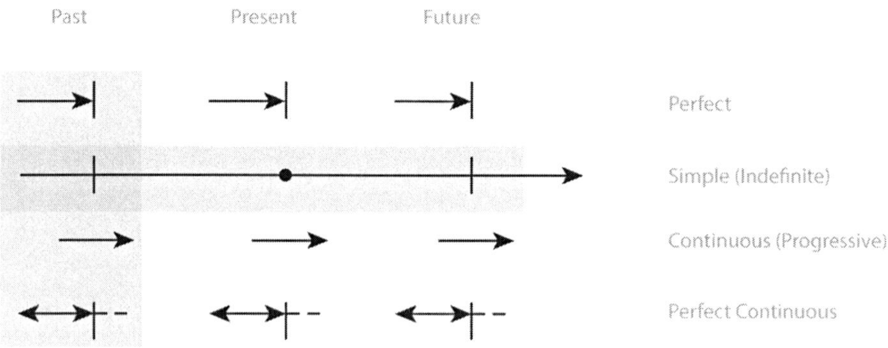

! For other Past Tenses (in both the Active and Passive Voices), you only need to learn the past form of one of the auxiliary verbs (*be* or *have*) but not of the main (action) verb. This will become clear very soon.

So! The II verb form (V2) — 'Past Form' (Past Tense)...

- Is only used to form a Past Simple Tense.
- And only for affirmative sentences (not for questions or negative forms).

Example: the verb *go.*

Its three forms are: *go* (I) — *went* (II) — *gone* (III).

For the Past tense:

Affirmative: *He went to school yesterday.*

Question: *Did he go to school yesterday?*

Negative: *He didn't go to school yesterday.*

We will discuss this in more detail later.

ESL learners have the most questions about form III (V3) — Past Participle.

open → *opened* → *opened*

Past Participle — III (V3)

The Past Participle is used:

1. To form tenses in the Perfect group (together with the verb *have)*.
    For example: *I have broken it.*

2. To form the Passive Voice (together with the verb *be*).
    For example: *It was broken.*

3. As an adjective.
    For example: *a broken leg.*

Think of it as an adjective — a word that describes a noun or pronoun (*description*).

Question: If they look the same, how do I know which one is a Past form and which one is a Past Participle?

I opened (the door)

I have opened (the door)

Answer: It's a Past form (II)

1. If there is a noun, name, or personal pronoun in front of it.
   For example: *I opened the door.*
2. Or if there is an adverb (a word that describes or gives more information about a verb, adjective, adverb, or phrase).
   For example: *I promptly opened the door*

I opened (the door)
I have opened (the door)

It's a Past Participle (III)

If in front of it there is "*have*" in one of its forms
(*have, has, had, will have, has been, had been, will have been*).
   For example: *It has been opened*

If in front of it there is "*be*" in one of its forms
(*am, is, are, was, were, will be*).
   For example: *It was opened.*

! Sometimes, the information is almost the same in both cases. The difference is that the focus of the message is on the action (*I did it*) in the first case, while the focus is on the result (*the door is now open*) in the second case.

In reality, there are not three verb forms but five, but most of us have completely forgotten this fact.

The two additional verb forms are the Present Participle (IV) and the Gerund (V).
Both forms end in *–ing*.

Verb Forms

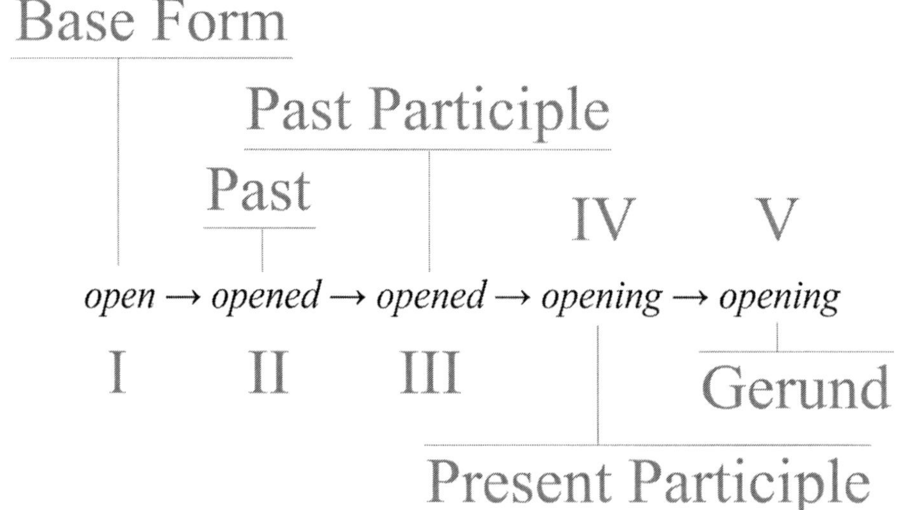

The Present Participle is used

1. As an adjective.
   Example: *The sleeping child.*

2. To form a tense of the Continuous group. But you can also see it as an adjective.
   Example: *She is sleeping. (She is currently in a state of sleep).*

The Gerund

Super easy! It's a noun formed from a verb by adding *–ing*.

Different sources say different things about Gerund. Some say it's still a verb, which is used as a noun. Let's go with this explanation.

run — verb; *running* — verb used as a noun
believe — verb; *believing* — verb used as a noun

–ed

If you see a regular verb ending in *–ed*, it's:

- Either a verb in the Past form (II).
- Or in the Past Participle form (III).

–ing

If you see a word ending in *–ing*, it's either Present Participle (IV) or a Gerund (V). So, basically, in a sentence, it can act as:

- A Verb (if it's a Present Participle)
- An Adjective (if it's a Present Participle)
- A Noun (if it's a Gerund)

Or it can be interpreted as one, depending on the context.

Let's review all five verb forms:

$$open \rightarrow opened \rightarrow opened \rightarrow opening \rightarrow opening$$

$$\text{I} \qquad \text{II} \qquad \text{III} \qquad \text{IV} \qquad \text{V}$$

I.   **Base Form** — The base form of a verb is identical to the dictionary entry. It does not bear any agreement, tense, or participle endings.

II.   **Past** — The Simple Past Tense is used to express an action completed at a specific time in the past (only once in the past).

III.   **Past Participle** — The Past Participle is used in the following ways:
1. To form tenses in the Perfect group (together with the verb *have*).
2. To form the Passive Voice (together with the verb *be*).
3. As an adjective to describe a noun or pronoun.

IV.   **Present Participle** — It can be used in the following ways:
1. As an adjective. Example: *The sleeping child.*
2. To form a tense of the Continuous group. But you can also see it as an adjective.

V.   **Gerund** — It is a noun formed from a verb by adding the ending *–ing*. Different sources say different things about it: some say it's still a verb, used as a noun.

Question: How do I create the different verb forms?

open → opened → opened → opening → opening

I   II   III   IV   V

I   Base form — *open*
II   Past tense — *opened*
III Past participle — *opened*   — add *–ed* (for regular verbs)
IV   Present participle — *opening*
V   Gerund — *opening*   — add *–ing* (for both regular and irregular verbs)

! Regular verbs — You create forms II and III simply by adding *–ed*.
Irregular verbs — Forms II and II are not created by adding *–ed*. Each form for each verb must be memorized.

So, for Irregular Verbs, the IV and V forms are:

Infinitive	Past Simple	Past Participle	Present Participle	Gerund
be	was / were	been	being	being
become	became	become	becoming	becoming
begin	began	begun	beginning	beginning
bring	brought	brought	bringing	bringing
buy	bought	bought	buying	buying
choose	chose	chosen	choosing	choosing
come	came	come	coming	coming
do	did	done	going	going
drink	drank	drunk	drinking	drinking
drive	drove	driven	driving	driving
eat	ate	eaten	eating	eating
fall	fell	fallen	falling	falling

And so on…

Question: When do I double a consonant before adding *–ing*?

Answer: A consonant is doubled if **a verb ends with a consonant** (but not *Y, X,* or *W*), **before which a vowel is stressed** in the pronunciation (but not a double vowel, like *OO, EA, AI,* or *EE*) **before which there is a consonant.**

This rule is called CVC or Consonant—Vowel—Consonant.

gét → getting   ópen → opening
rún → running   But!   remémber → remembering
stóp → stopping   feel → feeling
forgét → forgetting   read → reading

If the verb ends in *–ie*, it changes to *–y*. For example: *die → dying; lie → lying.*

If it ends with *–ic*, it changes to *–ick*. For example: *panic → panicking.*

In British English, in verbs ending in *L* (regardless of whether the vowel before is stressed or not), L is always doubled. For example: *travel → travelling, cancel → cancelling.*

In American English, the L is not doubled. For example: *traveling & canceling.*

In the example of *quit → quitting,* remember that the rule talks about sounds, not letters. The combination QU creates a consonant sound.

Question: When do I double a consonant before adding –ed?

Answer: Consonants double when you add other endings to words, like –er, –est, –ed.

But for now, only one is important, so we can learn how to form the Past (II) and Past Participle (III) verb forms.

The *CVC or Consonant—Vowel—Consonant* rule used with *–ing also* applies to *–ed*, with the same exceptions.

nód → nodded   *ópen → opened*
permít → permitted   **But!**   *cool → cooled*
stóp → stopped   *fix → fixed*
preférr → preferred   *snow → snowed*

Other rules for adding –ed:

You do not add a simple *–ed* to a word:

1. When a word ends with an *–e* or *–ee*, you only add *–d*.
    live → lived, close → closed

2. When a word ends with a *–y*, which has a consonant before it, you change *–y* with *–i*.
    cry → cried, study → studied

3. When a word ends in *–ic*, you change it to *–ick* before adding *–ed*.
    mimic → mimicked

Question: How am I supposed to memorize all this?

Answer: Actually, **it's better not to memorize it!**

The brain retains information with practice. It will more easily remember words you regularly use, not grammar rules.

When in doubt, just use a good dictionary.

Now, you should not have problems with verb forms.

The answer to question #3 (Which forms do English verbs have?)

I (Base Form),
II (Past),
III (Past Participle),
IV (Present Participle),
V (Gerund)

To review the answers to our questions:

- How many tenses does English have? — It has twelve tenses in the Active Voice and eight in the Passive Voice.
- What types of verbs does English have? — It has two: Main (Action) verbs and Helping or Auxiliary (Primary Auxiliary, Linking, Modal) verbs.
- What are the verb forms? — The forms are: I, II (Past), III (Past Participle), IV (Present Participle), and V (Gerund).

! Don't forget how to form the third-person singular:

In the Present Simple, for *he, she, it,* you add *–s* or *–es.*
For example: *I sleep — he sleeps*; *we go — it goes*

The verb *have* turns into *has.*
For example: *I have done — she has done*
I have been looking — he has been looking

Let's Start Studying the Chart for the Main 12 Tenses (Active Voice)

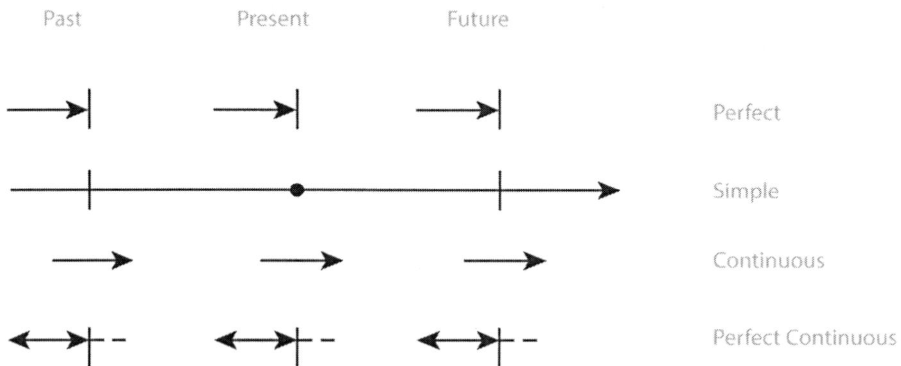

Why does the chart look like this?

The chart shows what the focus is in each case.

Different groups of tenses are used to emphasize different things in a message.

In the case of the Present Simple, it's a bit more complex.

Present Simple — The Present Simple describes a fact (point) or a repeating action (looks a bit like a circle).

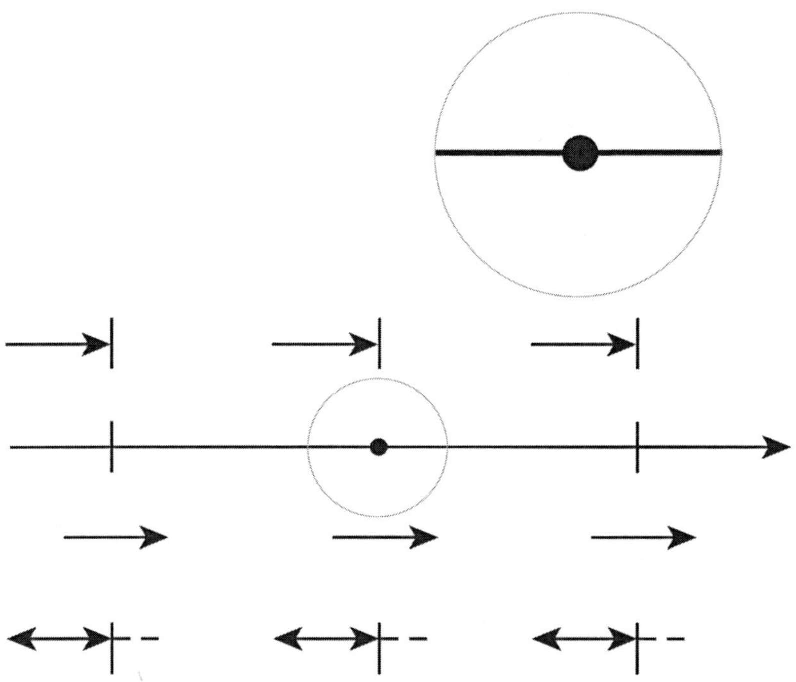

!   In other words, the Present Simple conveys that something is a fact, or that
    it keeps repeating.

Past and Future — Both the Past and Future tenses describe one action that takes place either in the past or in the future, respectively.

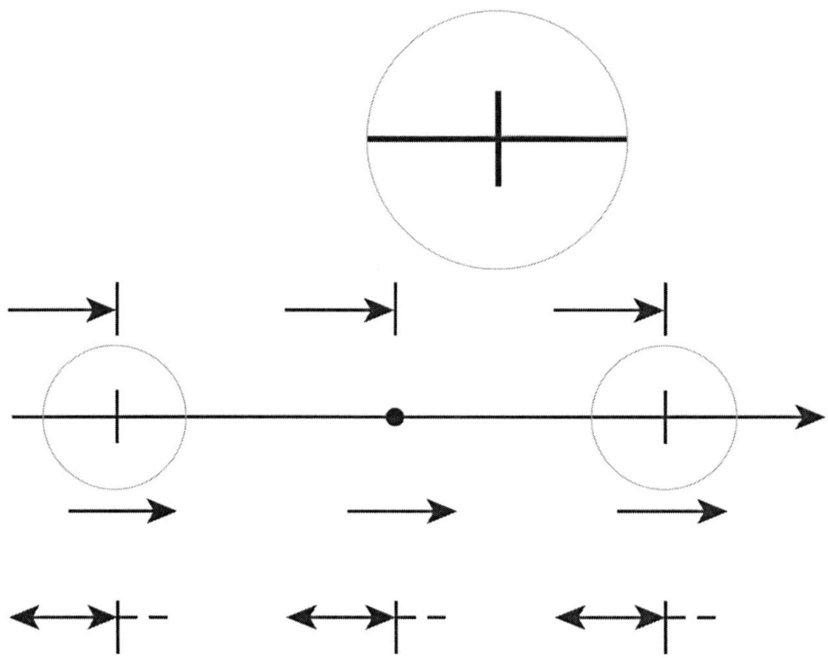

!   In other words, it expresses that one action happens at one particular moment in the past or the future — just once.

For example:
I bought those shoes in New York.
I will give him the book.

Simple

The group Simple is the only one
where the look of the marks differs

repeating actions or a fact
(of nature, of life)

action in the past
(one time)

action in the future
(one time)

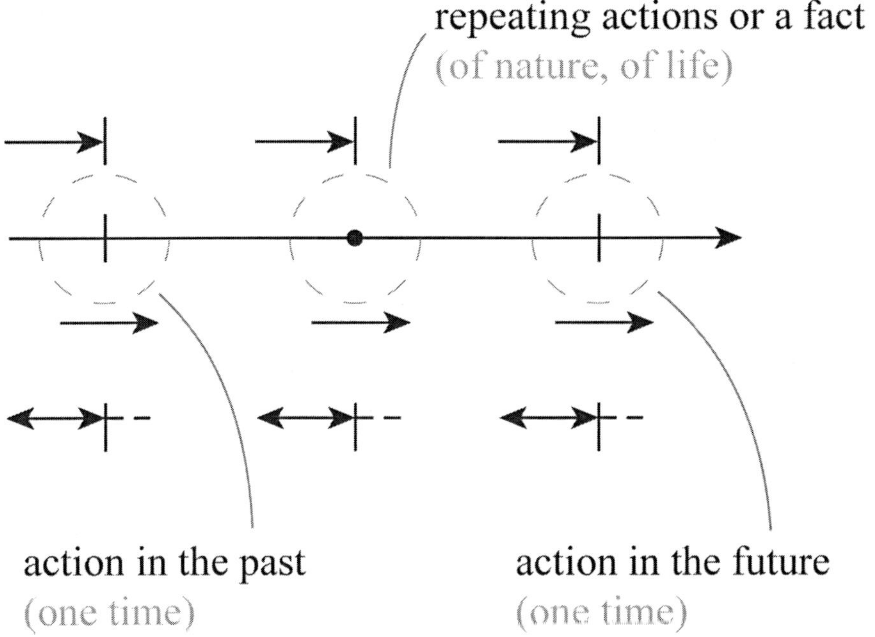

Perfect conveys the result of an action

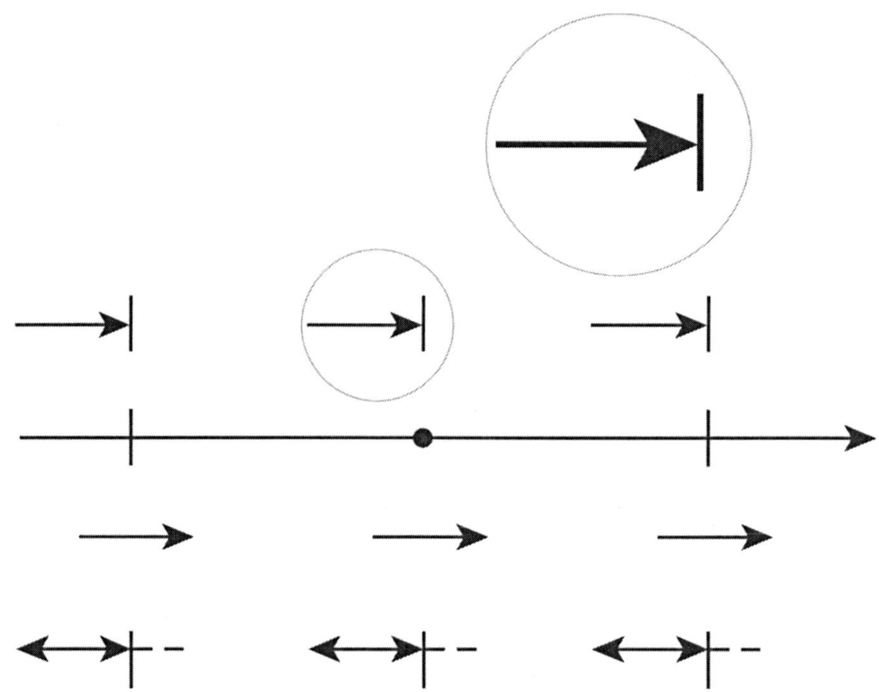

I have finished the report. (I have a result now.)
I had finished the report. (I had a result in the past.)
I will have finished the report. (I will have a result in the future.)

Continuous — Conveys movement, action, process

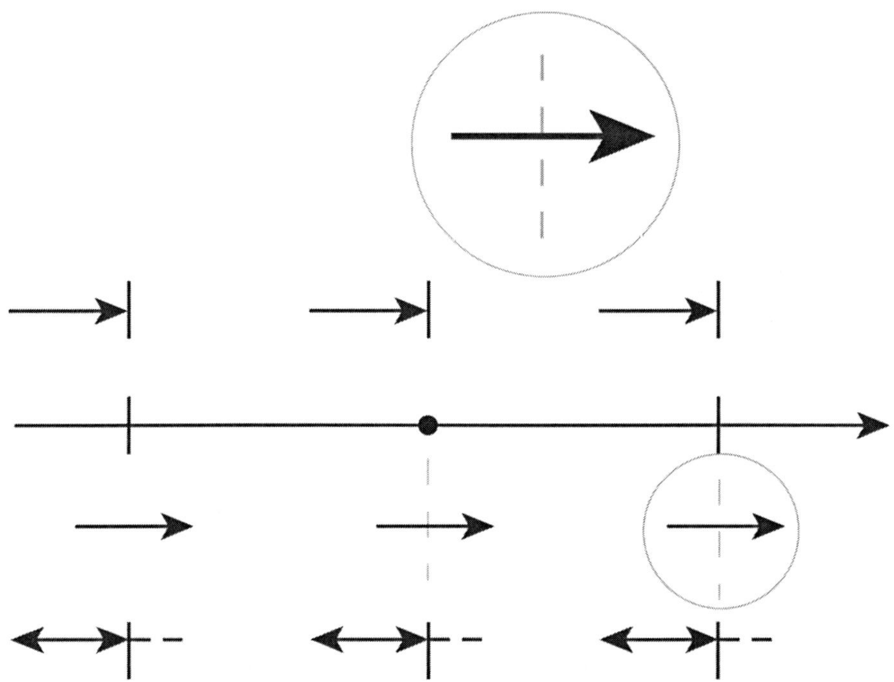

For example: *Tomorrow at 5 pm, I'll be flying home.*
(Tomorrow, at 5 pm, I'll be in the process of flying.)

Perfect-Continuous — The focus is on a time period

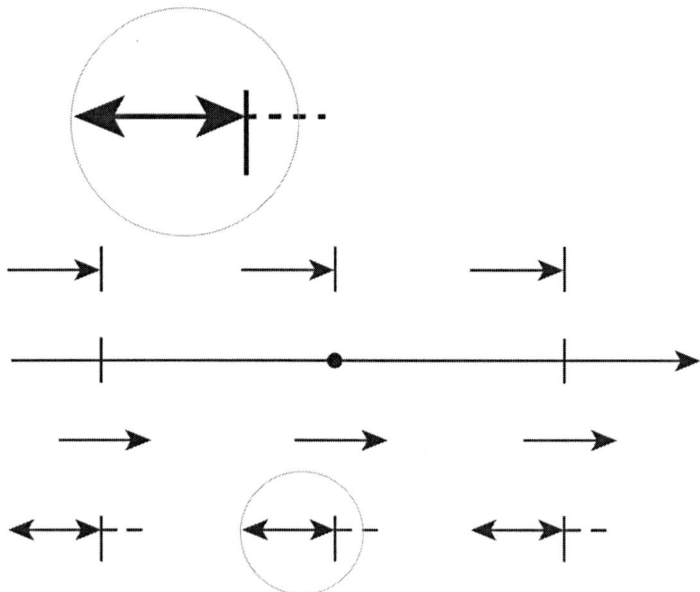

We've been looking all over for you —
We spent a lot of time doing this…

I've been working for this company for three years —
I spent a lot of time working for those bloodsuckers

Perfect-Continuous

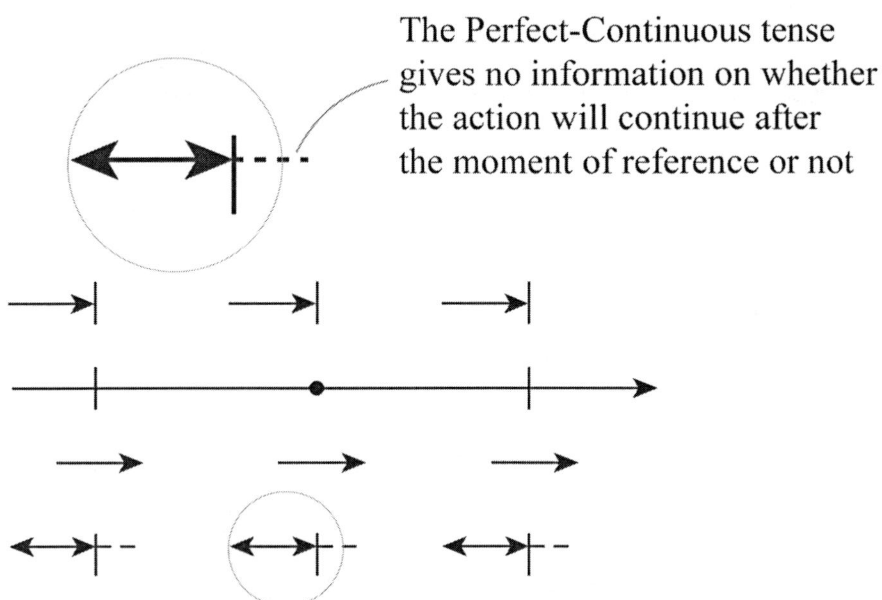

In other words, the action was happening (past),
is still happening (present),
or will be happening (future) for some time.
"By now," *"by a certain point in the past,"*
or *"by a certain point in the future."*

So!

Present Simple — A recurring action or fact of life

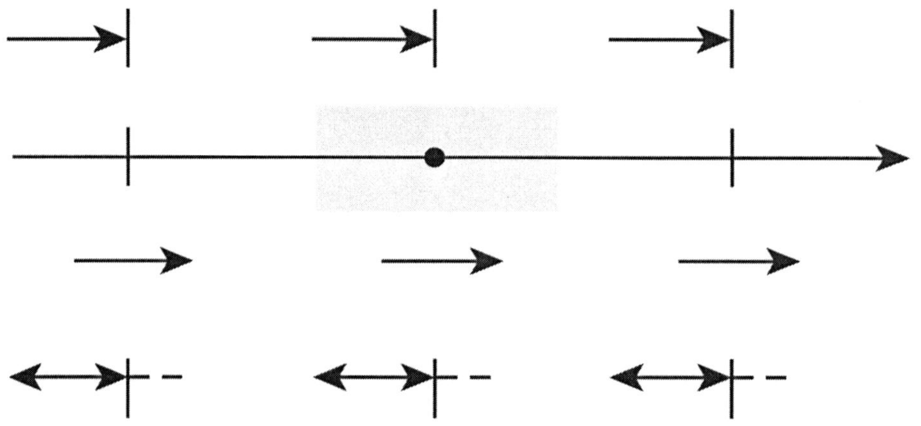

He's a fool! (It is a fact that he is a fool.)

The bus comes at 6 am. (According to the timetable, the bus comes at 6 am every day.)

Past and Future Simple — Only one action or event!

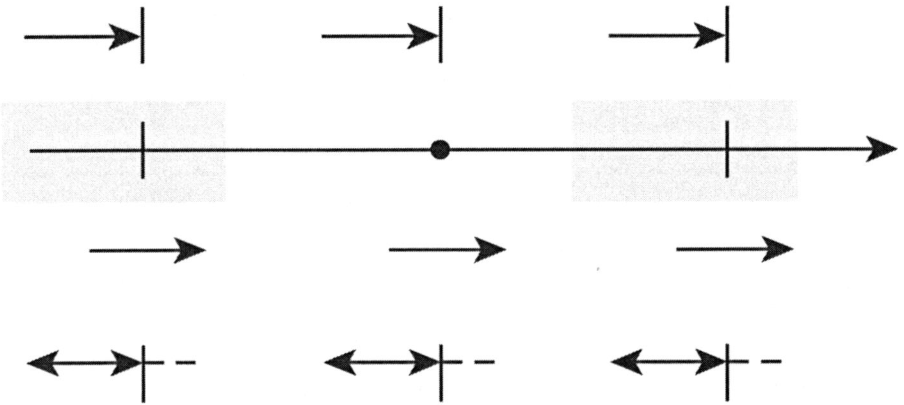

She took your keys. (She took your keys at an undefined time in the past.)
I'll call you tomorrow. (I will call you at an undefined time tomorrow.)

Perfect group — The focus is on the result

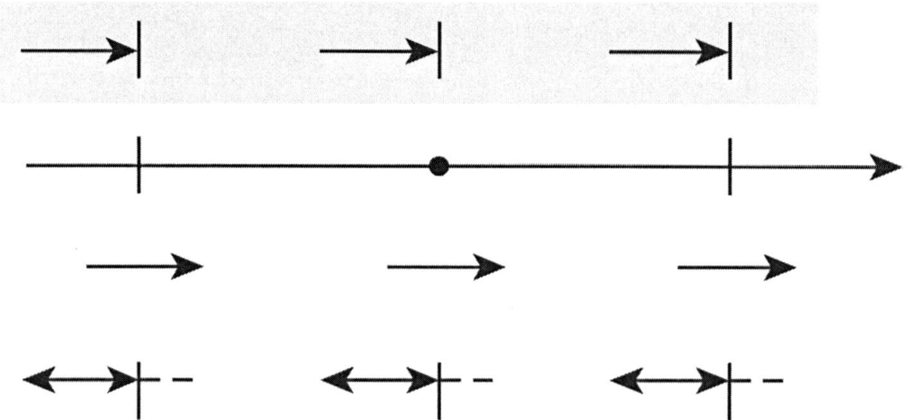

I will have fixed this by tomorrow. (The result is in the future.)
They had finished it by the time I came. (The result was completed in the past.)

Continuous group — The focus is on the process or progress

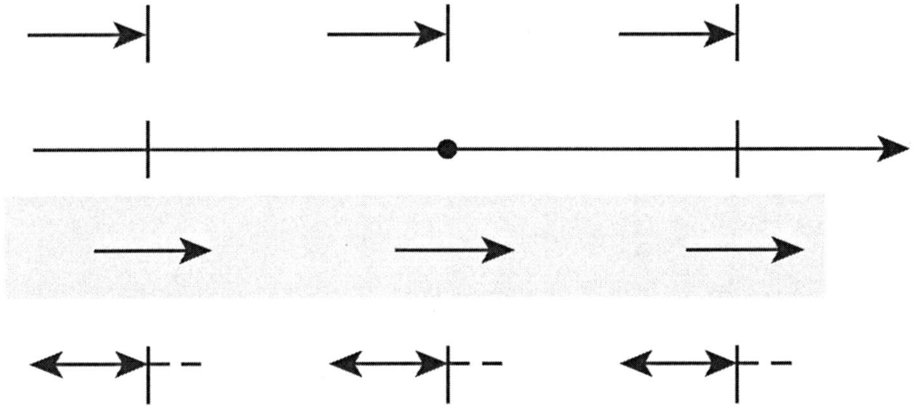

I'm eating. (I'm doing this action right now.)
I was watching TV yesterday evening. (Yesterday evening, I was in the process of watching TV.)

Perfect-Continuous Group — The focus on the time period (time spent doing something)

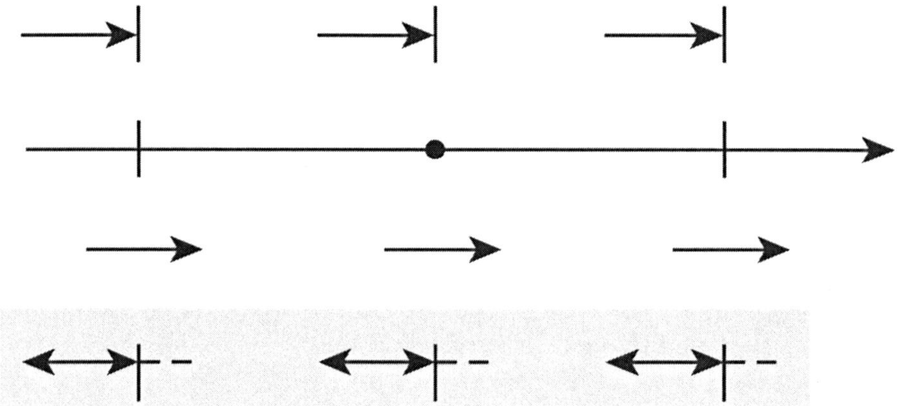

Once again!

regular action or a fact
result
process
time period
action
action

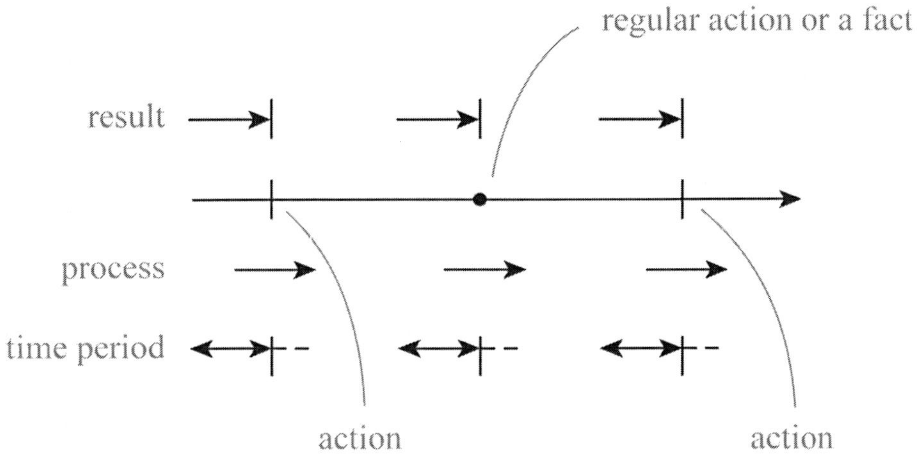

And now, the best part!

Within each group (Aspect), sentences are formed by following the same pattern.

See what changes in each group.

Past	Present	Future	
I had opened	*I have opened*	*I will have opened*	Perfect
I opened	*I open*	*I will open*	Simple
I was opening	*I am opening*	*I will be opening*	Continuous
I had been opening	*I have been opening*	*I will have been opening*	Perfect Continuous

In each group only the highlighted changes

	Past	Present	Future	
	I had opened	*I have opened*	*I will have opened*	Perfect
	I opened	*I open*	*I will open*	Simple
	I was opening	*I am opening*	*I will be opening*	Continuous
	I had been opening	*I have been opening*	*I will have been opening*	Perfect Continuous

had ← have → will have

	Past	Present	Future	
	I had opened	*I have opened*	*I will have opened*	Perfect
	I opened	*I open*	*I will open*	Simple
	I was opening	*I am opening*	*I will be opening*	Continuous
	I had been opening	*I have been opening*	*I will have been opening*	Perfect Continuous

opened ← open → will open

	Past	Present	Future	
	I had opened	*I have opened*	*I will have opened*	Perfect
	I opened	*I open*	*I will open*	Simple
	I was opening	*I am opening*	*I will be opening*	Continuous
	I had been opening	*I have been opening*	*I will have been opening*	Perfect Continuous

was ← am ([be]) → will be

	Past	Present	Future	
	I had opened	*I have opened*	*I will have opened*	Perfect
	I opened	*I open*	*I will open*	Simple
	I was opening	*I am opening*	*I will be opening*	Continuous
	I had been opening	*I have been opening*	*I will have been opening*	Perfect Continuous

had ← have → will have

What changes in the group Simple for the cases when we only have a linking verb '*be*'

Past	Present	Future	
			Perfect
I was an engineer	*I am an engineer*	*I will be an engineer*	Simple
			Continuous
			Perfect Continuous

was ← am ([be]) → *will be*

Can we describe those changes using formulas?

Let's put what changes in brackets, like this — [what changes]

+ a reminder
Have in the Past — *had,* in the future — *will have*

$$had \leftarrow have \rightarrow will\ have$$

Be (*am, are, is*) in the Past – *was,* in the Future – *will be*

$$was \leftarrow be \rightarrow will\ be$$

Perfect

Past	Present	Future	
I had opened	*I have opened*	*I will have opened*	Perfect
I opened	*I open*	*I will open*	Simple
I was opening	*I am opening*	*I will be opening*	Continuous
I had been opening	*I have been opening*	*I will have been opening*	Perfect Continuous

Formula: [have] + III (P.P.)

Simple

Past	Present	Future	
I *had* **opened**	I *have* **opened**	I *will have* **opened**	Perfect
I *opened*	I *open*	I *will open*	Simple
I *was* **opening**	I *am* **opening**	I *will be* **opening**	Continuous
I *had* **been opening**	I *have* **been opening**	I *will have* **been opening**	Perfect Continuous

Formula: [verb]

Continuous

Past	Present	Future	
I had opened	*I have opened*	*I will have opened*	Perfect
I opened	*I open*	*I will open*	Simple
I was opening	*I am opening*	*I will be opening*	Continuous
I had been opening	*I have been opening*	*I will have been opening*	Perfect Continuous

Formula: [be] + ing

Perfect Continuous

Past	Present	Future	
I had opened	*I have opened*	*I will have opened*	Perfect
I opened	*I open*	*I will open*	Simple
I was opening	*I am opening*	*I will be opening*	Continuous
I had been opening	*I have been opening*	*I will have been opening*	Perfect Continuous

Formula: [have] + been + ing

The Main Chart!

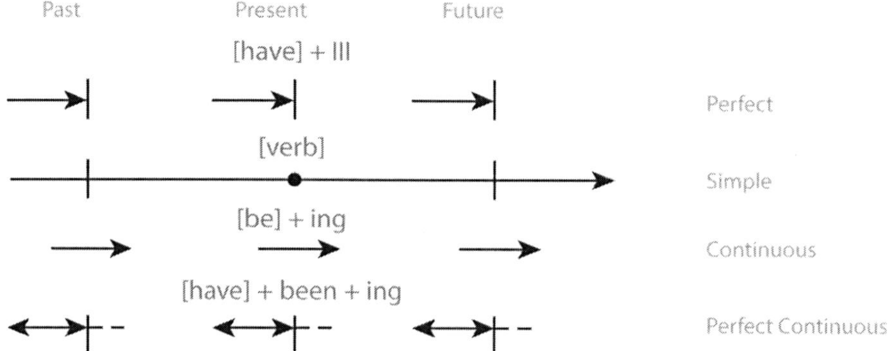

What changes?

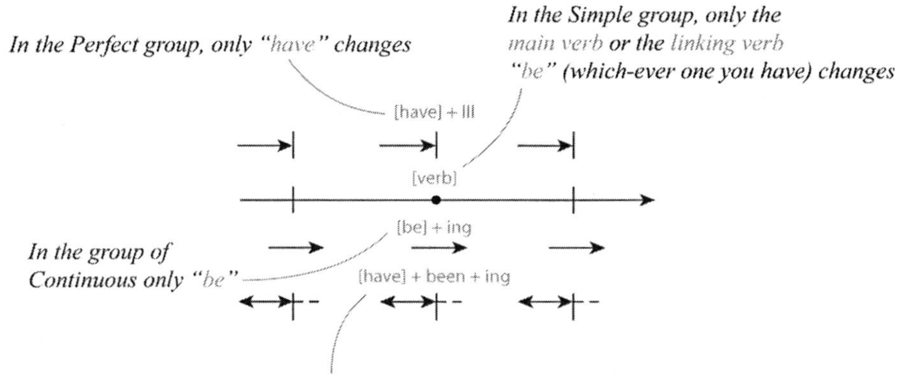

Hence the formulas for the Active Voice is as follows:

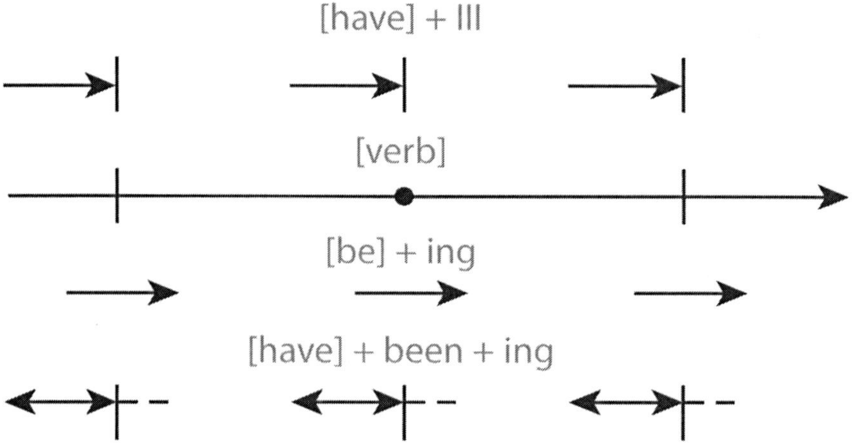

The easiest way to learn this is by memorizing one example sentence for each group — something relatable, something easy to remember.

The examples that I use are:

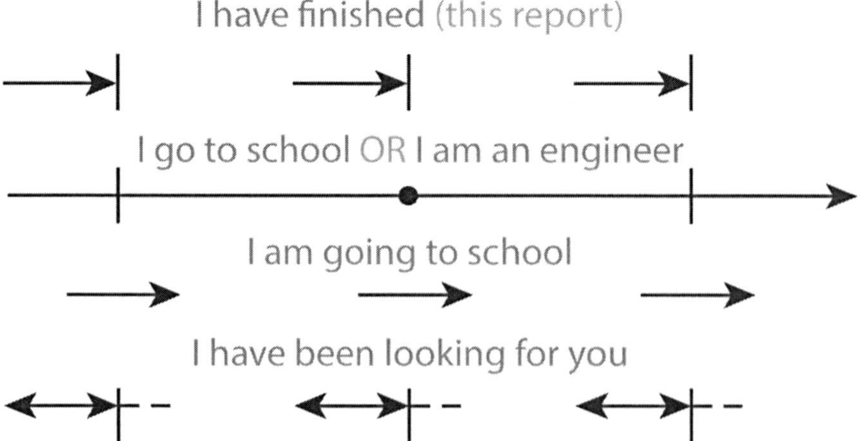

If I have forgotten the chart, I mentally spread out my examples along the timeline and generate the formulas again.

Past	Present	Future	
I had finished	*I have finished*	*I will have finished*	Perfect
I went to school	*I go to school*	*I will go to school*	Simple
I was going to school	*I'm going to school*	*I will be going to school*	Continuous
I had been looking for you	*I have been looking for you*	*I will have been looking for you*	Perfect Continuous

So, I get…

Past	Present	Future	
	[have] + III		Perfect
	[verb]		Simple
	[be] + ing		Continuous
	[have] + been + ing		Perfect Continuous

! *"Richard Of York Gave Battle In Vain."*

Or

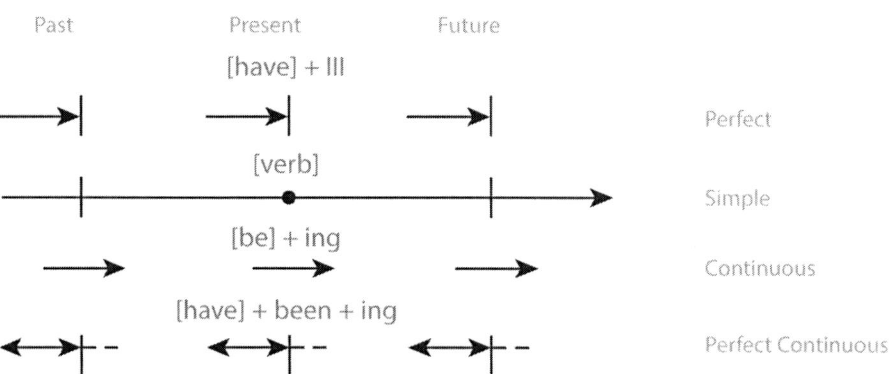

Let's look at different scenarios to understand the meaning of each tense.

Do you remember that each group of tenses looks at an action from a slightly different perspective?

Let me remind you!

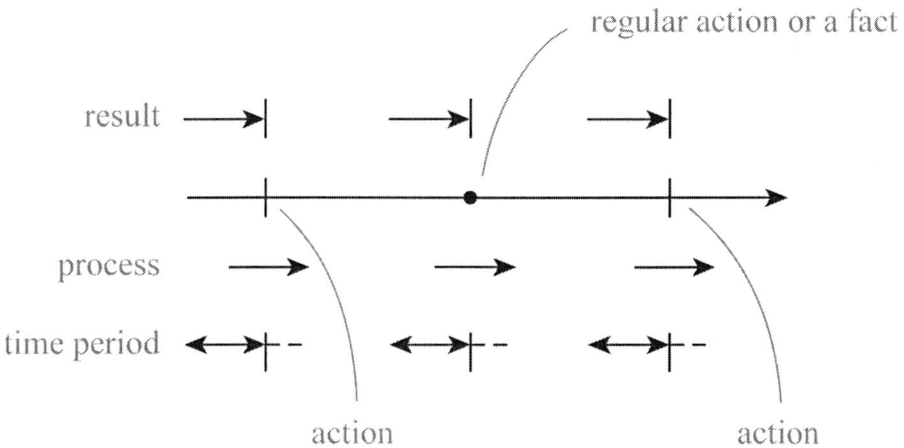

What do the different tenses convey?

Past	Present	Future	
The result we had by a certain moment in the past	*The result we have now*	*The result we will have by a certain moment in the future*	Perfect
The action happened in the past	*The action is recurring. It happens all the time*	*The action will happen in the future*	Simple
The process was happening at this moment in the past	*The process is happening right now*	*The process will be happening at this moment in the future*	Continuous
The action was happening until this moment in the past	*The action was happening until now*	*The action will be happening until this moment in the future*	Perfect Continuous

Let's use the verb '*open*' as an example:

Past	Present	Future	
I had opened	*I have opened*	*I will have opened*	Perfect
I opened	*I open*	*I will open*	Simple
I was opening	*I am opening*	*I will be opening*	Continuous
I had been opening	*I have been opening*	*I will have been opening*	Perfect Continuous

Present Simple

Past	Present	Future	
I had opened	*I have opened*	*I will have opened*	Perfect
I opened	*I open*	*I will open*	Simple
I was opening	*I am opening*	*I will be opening*	Continuous
I had been opening	*I have been opening*	*I will have been opening*	Perfect Continuous

I open. (This is an action I do regularly.)

I open this window every day. (Words like '*usually*' and '*every day*' are markers of the Present Simple.)

Future Simple

Past	*Present*	*Future*	
I had opened	*I have opened*	*I will have opened*	Perfect
I opened	*I open*	*I will open*	Simple
I was opening	*I am opening*	*I will be opening*	Continuous
I had been opening	*I have been opening*	*I will have been opening*	Perfect Continuous

I will open it. (I will do this action one time in the future.)

This tense often indicates that the decision to take this action was made just now. If it was pre-planned, the Present Continuous is used.

Past Simple

Past	Present	Future	
I had opened	*I have opened*	*I will have opened*	Perfect
I opened	*I open*	*I will open*	Simple
I was opening	*I am opening*	*I will be opening*	Continuous
I had been opening	*I have been opening*	*I will have been opening*	Perfect Continuous

I opened it. (I did this action one time in the past.)
Here, '*opened*' is a II (second) verb form (Past).

I opened the window before leaving.
The focus of this tense is action. Someone *did* something.

Present Perfect

Past	Present	Future	
I had opened	*I have opened*	*I will have opened*	Perfect
I opened	*I open*	*I will open*	Simple
I was opening	*I am opening*	*I will be opening*	Continuous
I had been opening	*I have been opening*	*I will have been opening*	Perfect Continuous

I have opened the window. (I have the *result* of the action already.)

Here, *'opened'* is a III (third) verb form (Past Participle).
The window is already open. The focus of this tense is a result.

Past Perfect

Past	Present	Future	
I had opened	*I have opened*	*I will have opened*	Perfect
I opened	*I open*	*I will open*	Simple
I was opening	*I am opening*	*I will be opening*	Continuous
I had been opening	*I have been opening*	*I will have been opening*	Perfect Continuous

I had opened. (At a certain moment in the past, I had the result. The window was open.)

By the time they came, I had already opened the window.

Future Perfect

<table>
<tr><td></td><td>Past</td><td>Present</td><td>Future</td><td></td></tr>
<tr><td>Perfect</td><td>I had opened</td><td>I have opened</td><td>I will have opened</td><td>Perfect</td></tr>
<tr><td></td><td>I opened</td><td>I open</td><td>I will open</td><td>Simple</td></tr>
<tr><td></td><td>I was opening</td><td>I am opening</td><td>I will be opening</td><td>Continuous</td></tr>
<tr><td></td><td>I had been opening</td><td>I have been opening</td><td>I will have been opening</td><td>Perfect Continuous</td></tr>
</table>

I will have opened. (At a certain moment in the future, I will have the result.)

I will have opened the window by the time they arrive.

Present Continuous

Past	Present	Future	
I had opened	*I have opened*	*I will have opened*	Perfect
I opened	*I open*	*I will open*	Simple
I was opening	*I am opening*	*I will be opening*	Continuous
I had been opening	*I have been opening*	*I will have been opening*	Perfect Continuous

I am opening the window. (The action is taking place right now.)

Future Continuous

Past	Present	Future	
I had opened	*I have opened*	*I will have opened*	Perfect
I opened	*I open*	*I will open*	Simple
I was opening	*I am opening*	*I will be opening*	Continuous
I had been opening	*I have been opening*	*I will have been opening*	Perfect Continuous

I will be opening. (At a certain moment in the future I will be in the process of opening…)

By the time you graduate from school, I'll be opening my second restaurant.

Past Continuous

Past	Present	Future	
I had opened	*I have opened*	*I will have opened*	Perfect
I opened	*I open*	*I will open*	Simple
I was opening	*I am opening*	*I will be opening*	Continuous
I had been opening	*I have been opening*	*I will have been opening*	Perfect Continuous

I was opening. (At a certain point in the past, I was in the process of opening…)

I was opening the champagne bottle when it exploded in my hands.

Present Perfect-Continuous

Past	Present	Future	
I had opened	*I have opened*	*I will have opened*	Perfect
I opened	*I open*	*I will open*	Simple
I was opening	*I am opening*	*I will be opening*	Continuous
I had been opening	*I have been opening*	*I will have been opening*	Perfect Continuous

I have been opening. (It has been a while since I started opening…)

Future Perfect-Continuous

Past	Present	Future	
I had opened	*I have opened*	*I will have opened*	Perfect
I opened	*I open*	*I will open*	Simple
I was opening	*I am opening*	*I will be opening*	Continuous
I had been opening	*I have been opening*	*I will have been opening*	Perfect Continuous

I will have been opening. (At a certain point in the future, I will have been in the process of opening for quite a while.)

Past Perfect-Continuous

Past	Present	Future	
I had opened	*I have opened*	*I will have opened*	Perfect
I opened	*I open*	*I will open*	Simple
I was opening	*I am opening*	*I will be opening*	Continuous
I had been opening	*I have been opening*	*I will have been opening*	Perfect Continuous

I had been opening. (At a certain point in the past, I had been in the process of opening it for quite a while.)

Past Simple & Present Perfect

Sometimes, the Past Simple and Present Perfect can be used interchangeably. But because of the different shades of meaning that they bear, sometimes the message changes depending on which one you use.

Past	Present	Future	
I had opened	*I have opened*	*I will have opened*	Perfect
I opened	*I open*	*I will open*	Simple
I was opening	*I am opening*	*I will be opening*	Continuous
I had been opening	*I have been opening*	*I will have been opening*	Perfect Continuous

Past Simple — one action completed in the past.

Example: *I watched a movie yesterday.* (The focus is on the action. I did watch the movie.)

Present Perfect — the action was completed in the past, and now there is a result.

Example: *I have watched this movie.* (The focus is on the result, not on the action.) Result: *I have seen the movie BEFORE.* Maybe I have seen it many times — this doesn't matter. What matters is that I know its plot.

Have & Get

The verb *get* has many meanings. But to simplify, its main meaning is 'to *receive'*.

The verb forms are: *get* → *got* → *got* (*gotten* – in American English) → *getting* → *getting*.

So, in order to say that you *have* something, you may say:

1. ***I have*** — (Present Simple)
2. **I have had** — *have + III of the verb have* (Present Perfect)
3. ***I have got*** *(I've got)* — *have + III of the verb get* (Present Perfect) — I have it in my possession. (In American English: *I've gotten*, but *I've got* is a more widely accepted form.)
4. ***I got*** — *II of the verb get* (Past Simple) — *get* sometimes replaces the verb *have* in so-called Causative Forms.

Example: *I need to get the washing machine fixed.* (This is the same as: I need to have the washing machine fixed.)

Present Perfect & Present Perfect Continuous

	Past	Present	Future	
	I had opened	*I have opened*	*I will have opened*	Perfect
	I opened	*I open*	*I will open*	Simple
	I was opening	*I am opening*	*I will be opening*	Continuous
	I had been opening	*I have been opening*	*I will have been opening*	Perfect Continuous

Sometimes, the Present Perfect and the Present Perfect Continuous can be used interchangeably.

Examples:
— *How long have you studied Russian?*
— *How long have you been studying Russian?*

But!

! If you need to stress that the action is complete and there is a result, then choose the Present Perfect.

If you need to stress that the action or process was a long one, then choose the Present Perfect Continuous.

Had had

One of my schoolday nightmares was the combination *had had*.

But it stops being scary the moment you realize that it's just the verb *have* in the Past Perfect — I had it before. (at a certain moment in the past).

Example: *Last Saturday I just wanted to relax because I had had a busy week.*

The formula for the whole Perfect group: [have] + III

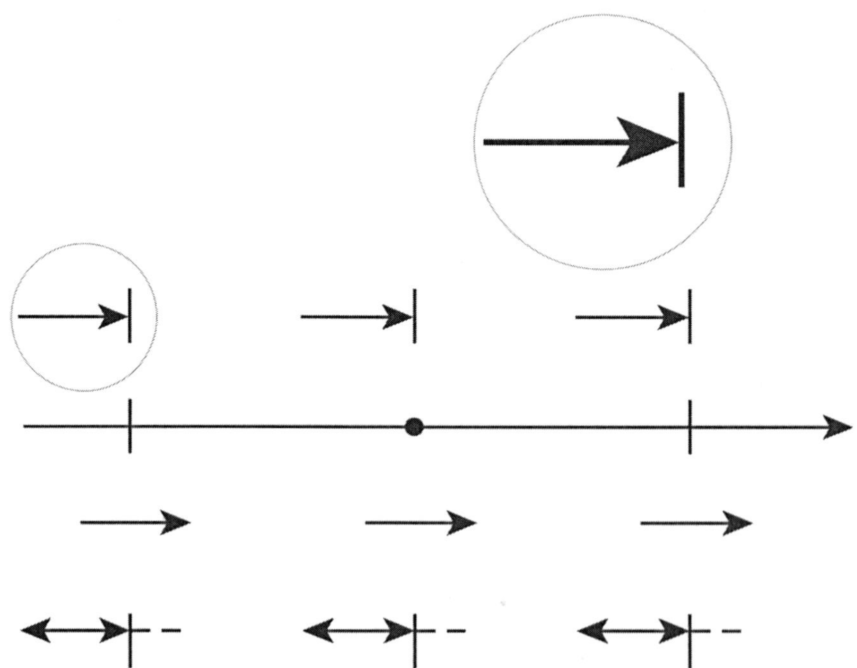

The first *had* is an auxiliary verb (the second form of the verb *have*), and the second *had* is the main verb (the third form of the verb *have*).

Past	Present	Future	
I had had my breakfast	*I have had my breakfast*	*I will have had my breakfast*	Perfect

Meaning

Past	Present	Future
I had it by this moment	*I have it by now*	*I will have it by this moment*

For the third-person singular:

Past	Present	Future	
he had had...	*he has had...*	*he will have had...*	Perfect

Had × 11

This is a little trick that English-language teachers love — a sentence used to demonstrate lexical ambiguity and the necessity for punctuation, which serves as a substitute for intonation, stress, and pauses in speech. It also employs the combination *had had.*

James while John had had had had had had had had had had a better effect on the teacher.

Meaning:

The sentence is talking about two students, John and James, who were asked on a test to describe a man who had suffered from a cold in the past. John wrote, "*The man had a cold,*" which the teacher marks as incorrect. James wrote the correct, "*The man had had a cold.*" Since James's answer was right, it had had a better effect on the teacher.

The sentence is easier to understand with punctuation and emphasis:
James, while John had had '*had*', had had '*had had*'; '*had had*' had had a better effect on the teacher.

Asking a Question

Reminder: We use the full form instead of a contraction for emphasis.

Example: "*I do not smoke*" instead of "*I don't smoke.*"

Another way to emphasize something is by adding an extra verb *do*.

We will be using this method a lot in this course. It helps you understand how questions and negatives can be formed.

— *I know how to type.*
— *I do know how to type.*

I do watch — he did watch — they do do

Absolutely legitimate phrases:

- *I do watch* — instead of: *I watch*
- *he did watch* — instead of: *he watched* — main
- *they do do (that)* — instead of: *they do* — main

auxiliary

main

We just stress the message. And if we were to translate those additional verbs '*do*', we would probably add the word 'really', as in 'this is true'!

How do I form a question?

You use an Inversion (you change the order of the words).

You have done → *Have you done?*

The easiest way to explain it is this:

You move your auxiliary verb to the front of a sentence. If you do not have an auxiliary verb, you add it and then move it to the front.

If you are adding an auxiliary verb, it will always be '*do*' in the Present or Past tense.

'*do*' (for the Present); '*does*' (for the Present, third-person singular); '*did*' (for the Past)

— *You have to do this*

↓

— *You do have to do this*

↓

— *Do you have to do this?*

1. The easiest way to explain is this: You move your auxiliary verb to the front of a sentence. If you do not have an auxiliary verb, you add it, and then you move it.

2. Strictly speaking, we do not necessarily move an auxiliary verb. Sometimes, it's the linking verb *be* in one of its forms (*am, is, are, was, were*). **Other linking verbs are not moved.**

She is happy. (statement) — *Is she happy?* (question)
He was an engineer. (statement) — *Was he an engineer?* (question)

3. Or you move the Modal verbs *will* (*would*)*, *can* (*could*), *may* (*might*), *must*. Other modal verbs are not moved. And if so, See rule #1.

You never move main verbs.
So, see rule #1.

!   * — The verb "*will*" (and its Past form would) is a Modal verb, not an auxiliary.

It's kind of funny with the verb HAVE…

have can be an auxiliary or a main verb.

- Example: *You have repaired my car.* (You got it fixed).
  Here, *have* is an auxiliary verb; the main verb in this sentence is *repair* in its third form (III).
- Example: *You have a car.* (You own a car).
  Here, *have* is the main verb.

Have (used as an auxiliary verb)

If *have* is an auxiliary verb, you form the statement like this:

You have repaired my car.

If you want to form a question, you use the rule about moving the auxiliary verb to the front of a sentence.

Have you repaired my car?

Have (used as a main verb)

When *have* is a main verb, you form the statement this way:

You have a car. (You own a car.)

To form a question, it used to be a norm to move *have* to the front of the sentence.

— *Have* **you a car?** (question)

While the above is grammatically correct, in modern American English, the new norm is to add an extra auxiliary verb *do*.

— *Do you have* **a car?**

you have a car (statement)

↓

you do have a car (stressed statement)

↓

do you have a car? (question)

Quick reference about 'what to move'.

	Past	Present	Future	
Perfect	*had*	*[have]*	
Simple	*was, were, did*	*[be], [do]*	*will*
Continuous	*was, were*	*[be]*	
Perfect Continuous	*had*	*[have]*	

!   [have] — *have* for *I, you, we, they* (but *has* for *he, she, it*)

     [be] — *I am, you are, he is, we are, they are*

     [do] — *do* for *I, you, we, they* (but *does* for *he, she, it*)

The 'Extra' Auxiliary Verb

! You can use an extra auxiliary verb *do* for additional emphasis:
— *I did wash the dishes!* (I really washed the dishes!)

We can add '*do*' or '*did*' for extra stress only in the Present Simple and Past Simple tenses.

There's a rule, which I call "Do it just once!"

And I divide this rule into two sub-rules:

1) "He does it just once."
2) "I did it just once."

The 'He-Does-It-Just-Once' Rule

In the third-person singular in the Present Perfect, if we add an extra *do* (to emphasize or form a question), the main verb loses the third-person singular indicator at the end. In other words, it loses its *–s* or *–es*.

We indicate the third-person singular only once, with only one verb.

Example:
He watches → *He does watch* (He really watches!)

What happened here? We added an extra *do*. But we have *he* (third-person singular), so *do* becomes *does* — *does* already shows that we are talking about the third-person singular. So, the main verb has nothing to prove. We have already indicated the third-person singular.

In short: The added *do* became *does*, and *does* already shows us everything regarding the third-person singular.

He watches → *He does watch* (He really watches!)
We indicate the third-person singular only once, with only one verb.

The 'I-Did-It-Just-Once' Rule

If we add an extra *do* to a Past Simple tense, it becomes *did* (because it happened in the past) — *did* steals the Past tense indication from the main verb.

So! We indicate the past only once, with only one verb!
(With the auxiliary verb *did*)

Example:
I watched (statement) → *I did watch* (stressed statement)

What happened here? We added an extra *do*, which became *did* (because the action happened in the past). That *did* 'steals' the Past tense indication from the main verb, so *watched* becomes *watch.*

I watched → *I did watch* (I really watched!)
We indicate the past only once, with only one verb!

The 'Do-it-Just-Once' rule is used only for the two highlighted tenses:

Past	Present	Future	
he had watched	he has watched	he will have watched	Perfect
he watched → he did watch	he watches → he does watch	he will watch	Simple
he was watching	he is watching	he will be watching	Continuous
he had been watching	he has been watching	he will have been watching	Perfect Continuous

! For all other tenses, we always have an auxiliary verb to move forward…
to form a question.

So! How Do We Form a Question?

Past	Present	Future	
he had watched	*he has watched*	*he will have watched*	Perfect
he watched → **he did watch**	*he watches* → **he does watch**	*he will watch*	Simple
he was watching	*he is watching*	*he will be watching*	Continuous
he had been watching	*he has been watching*	*he will have been watching*	Perfect Continuous

To turn a statement into a question, we move an auxiliary verb to the front of the sentence — just one word!

If there's no auxiliary verb (Example: *I watch*), insert it (the verb *do*), and move that instead!

In the case of '*He watches*', you use the 'He-Does-It-Just-Once' rule. You add *do* (it's a third-person singular), so *do* becomes *does*. Since *does* already indicates the third-person singular, *watches* becomes *watch*.

We had: *he watches* → we get: *he does watch*.

In the case of '*I watched*', you use the 'Do-It-Just-Once' rule — you put the auxiliary verb *do*. *Do* turns into *did* (because the action happened in the past. Since *did* already indicates the Past tense, *watched* becomes *watch*.

We had: *he watched* → we get: *he did watch*.

To form a question, we put an auxiliary verb at the beginning of a sentence.

Past	Present	Future	
had he had watched?	*has he has watched?*	*will he will have watched?*	Perfect
he watched → did he did watch?	*he watches → does he does watch?*	*will he will watch?*	Simple
was he was watching?	*is he is watching?*	*will he will be watching?*	Continuous
had he had been watching?	*has he has been watching?*	*will he will have been watching?*	Perfect Continuous

Or with '*be*' for the Simple group…

Past	Present	Future	
			Perfect
was I was an engineer?	*am I am an engineer?*	*will I will be an engineer?*	Simple
			Continuous
			Perfect Continuous

! Remember: you only need to move one word (!)
(look at the Future tense: we move *will*, not *will be*)

So! Questions in English are mostly formed through an Inversion (by changing the word order), not through intonation.

Questions formed through intonation are more often used in Russian, Spanish, or French. Nevertheless, as your experience with English tenses and questions grows, you'll start noticing some common situations and phrases in which using intonation to ask a question is not only allowed but also advisable.

There are no strict rules about that. It'll just come to you when you start noticing how native English speakers talk.

Got it? Good!

See what I did there?

More examples of using Inversion:

Direct word order	Using inversion for additional stress
If I had known it, I would have helped him	*Had I known it, I would have helped him*
The driver asked us where we wanted to go	*"Where to?" asked the driver*
She was so mad!	*Oh boy, was she mad!*
How beautiful these flowers are!	*How beautiful are these flowers!*
You don't know that	*That you don't know!*
I have never felt such fear before	*Never before have I felt such fear*

How Do You Form a Negative?

Past	Present	Future	
I had not watched	*I have not watched*	*I will not have watched*	Perfect
I watched → I did not watch	*I watch → I do not watch*	*I will not watch*	Simple
I was not watching	*I am not watching*	*I will not be watching*	Continuous
I had not been watching	*I have not been watching*	*I will not have been watching*	Perfect Continuous

! To form a negative, you put *not* after an auxiliary verb (or modal, or linking verb). If there's no auxiliary verb, first you add it, and then you put *not* after it.

Remember to use contractions in spoken language.

Past	Present	Future	
I hadn't watched	*I haven't watched*	*I won't have watched***	Perfect
I watched → I didn't watch	*I watch → I don't watch*	*I won't watch*	Simple
I was not watching	*I am not watching**	*I won't be watching*	Continuous
I hadn't been watching	*I haven't been watching*	*I won't have been watching*	Perfect Continuous

! * *am not* is not contracted, but you can contract *I am* — so, *I am not* = *I'm not*

** *won't* is the contraction for *will not* — so, *won't* = *will not* (try to master its pronunciation [wəʊnt])

'Do-It-Just-Once' Rule — Recap

For practice, run this chain of sentences:

affirmative sentence → affirmative with an extra auxiliary verb '*do*' (if needed) → *question* **(move your auxiliary verb to the front of your sentence) →** *negative* **(put '*not*' after your auxiliary verb)**

He watches → He does watch → Does he watch? → He doesn't watch
He watched → He did watch → Did he watch? → He didn't watch

Affirmative → question → negative

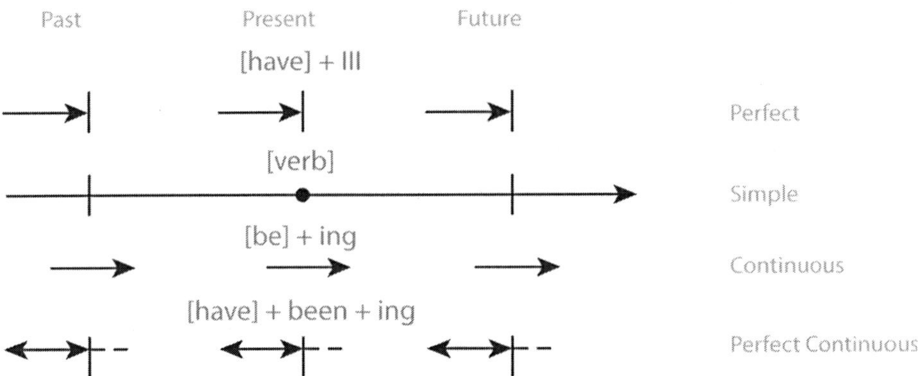

When you practice, take one verb and run it through all 12 tenses in all relevant forms — as an affirmative statement, as a question, and as a negative.

Using English Tenses

Speaking about the present (current events)

Past	Present	Future	
I had watched	*I have watched*	*I will have watched*	Perfect
I watched	*I watch*	*I will watch*	Simple
I was watching	*I am watching*	*I will be watching*	Continuous
I had been watching	*I have been watching*	*I will have been watching*	Perfect Continuous

! To talk about something that is going on right now, we use the Present Continuous.

This one is used only for repeating actions and facts of life.

	Past	Present	Future	
	I had watched	*I have watched*	*I will have watched*	Perfect
	I watched	*I watch*	*I will watch*	Simple
	I was watching	*I am watching*	*I will be watching*	Continuous
	I had been watching	*I have been watching*	*I will have been watching*	Perfect Continuous

A fact of life: *Light travels at almost 300,000 kilometers per second.*
A fact at the present moment: *I'm forty years old.*
Something that happens regularly: *She plays football.*

The fact that the Present Simple is the most commonly used tense proves that people tend to state the obvious.

Funnily enough, the Present Simple is not used to describe the present. It is often used to describe future or past events. We'll talk about that in a bit.

Speaking About the Past

	Past	Present	Future	
	I had watched	I have watched	I will have watched	Perfect
	I watched	I watch	I will watch	Simple
	I was watching	I am watching	I will be watching	Continuous
	I had been watching	I have been watching	I will have been watching	Perfect Continuous

■ — *more often*   ▨ — *less often*

Talking about the past: The three most commonly-used tenses

	Past	Present	Future	
	I had watched	I have watched	I will have watched	Perfect
	I watched	I watch	I will watch	Simple
	I was watching	I am watching	I will be watching	Continuous
	I had been watching	I have been watching	I will have been watching	Perfect Continuous

Past Simple — used to describe something that happened in the past. Example: *I lost my wallet.*

Present Perfect — used to describe something that affects the present moment (it describes the result of an action that we have at the moment). Example: *I've lost my wallet.* (I do not have it anymore.)

Past Continuous — used to describe an action that someone was doing or an event that was happening at a particular time. Example: *I lost my wallet yesterday when I was going to the office.* (*lost my wallet* — time marker, *I was going* — action)

"Fancy" tenses used to describe the past

Past	Present	Future	
I had watched	*I have watched*	*I will have watched*	Perfect
I watched	*I watch*	*I will watch*	Simple
I was watching	*I am watching*	*I will be watching*	Continuous
I had been watching	*I have been watching*	*I will have been watching*	Perfect Continuous

You can only use these tenses together with the Past Simple (either mentioned directly or in the subtext). The Past Continuous is also a fancy tense, but it is used much more often than Past Perfect or Past Perfect Continuous.

How to talk about the past

Past	Present	Future	
I had watched	*I have watched*	*I will have watched*	Perfect
I watched	*I watch*	*I will watch*	Simple
I was watching	*I am watching*	*I will be watching*	Continuous
I had been watching	*I have been watching*	*I will have been watching*	Perfect Continuous

! We need to explain this particular example — when and how you can use those tenses to talk about the past.

Talking about the past — Present Simple

The Present Simple can be used to describe the past in the following cases:

- Newspaper headlines (in some cases, this is the general journalistic style)

Example: *Real Madrid wins against Manchester United.*

- So-called Historical Present (or Dramatic Present), which is used to make stories more vivid and engaging by bringing past actions into the immediate present (by placing you into the story).

Example: *1945: the war in Europe comes to an end.*

- It is also used when telling a joke (to get the same effect of putting a listener inside the story).

Example: *A horse walks into a bar. The barman says, "Why the long face?"* (a play on words)

- Retelling movies, books, or life anecdotes — the Present Simple is used for events in the story, and the Present Continuous is used for background events or actions.

Example: *So, I walk into this shop, and I see this man with a gun in his hand.*

Using the Present Continuous to talk about the past

As mentioned above, the Present Continuous can be used for retelling movies, books, or life anecdotes. The Present Simple is used for events in the story, and the Present Continuous is used for background events or actions.

Example: *The other day, I'm just walking down the street when suddenly this man comes to me and asks me to lend him some money. Well, he's carrying a big stick and looks a bit dangerous, so I'm wondering what to do.*

Speaking About the Future

Past	Present	Future	
I had watched	*I have watched*	*I will have watched*	Perfect
I watched	*I watch*	*I will watch*	Simple
I was watching	*I am watching*	*I will be watching*	Continuous
I had been watching	*I have been watching*	*I will have been watching*	Perfect Continuous

■ —— *more often*　　□ —— *less often*

When we speak about the future, we use…

Past	Present	Future	
I had watched	*I have watched*	*I will have watched*	Perfect
I watched	*I watch*	*I will watch*	Simple
I was watching	*I am watching*	*I will be watching*	Continuous
I had been watching	*I have been watching*	*I will have been watching*	Perfect Continuous

Present Continuous — used when the action was planned.

Example: *I'm going to this new play at the Bolshoy Theater next weekend.* (planned)

Future Simple — used when you have just decided to do something now.

Example: *I'll join you if they still have tickets.* (last minute, not pre-planned)

Using the Present Simple to describe the future

Past	Present	Future	
I had watched	*I have watched*	*I will have watched*	Perfect
I watched	*I watch*	*I will watch*	Simple
I was watching	*I am watching*	*I will be watching*	Continuous
I had been watching	*I have been watching*	*I will have been watching*	Perfect Continuous

The Present Simple can be used to describe the future when you are sure that the event will take place (if you are certain that it will happen).

Examples:

She comes next Friday.

He finishes his five-year term in June.

'Fancy' tenses to describe the future

Past	Present	Future	
I had watched	*I have watched*	*I will have watched*	Perfect
I watched	*I watch*	*I will watch*	Simple
I was watching	*I am watching*	*I will be watching*	Continuous
I had been watching	*I have been watching*	*I will have been watching*	Perfect Continuous

! These fancy tenses are only used if tied to a time marker — to the Future Simple

English Tenses — Frequency of Use

Past	Present	Future	
1.2 %	6.0 %	0.2 %	Perfect
19.7 %	57.1 %	8.5 %	Simple
1.4 %	5.1 %	<0.1 %	Continuous
<0.1 %	0.7 %	<0.1 %	Perfect Continuous

There are many different studies, and they all show the same percentages, more or less. But! Please note that these studies are mostly based on scientific or journalistic texts, not real-life speech.

Do not ignore the less frequently-used tenses

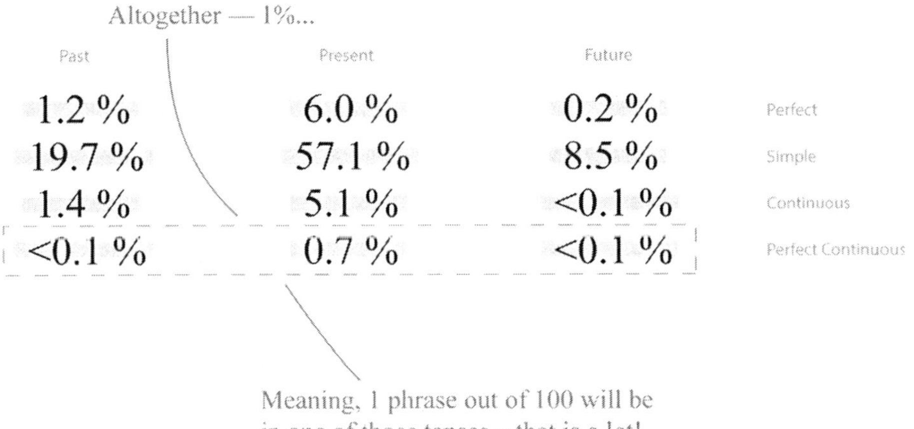

Don't tell yourself that you can do with only 3–4 tenses. Besides, it's only one verb that changes in each group.

In the case of the Perfect Continuous, only the verb [have] changes:

had ← have (has) → will have.

Passive Voice

In the Passive Voice, the subject receives an action
— *The door was opened (by me)*

Here, "*me*" is the so-called Agent of the action.
Basically, it indicates who did it.
You may add an Agent in your phrase, or you may omit him or her

Why do we need the Passive Voice?

1. **To bring some variety to our speech** — if we talked using only the Active Voice, our speech would be too dry and monotonous.

2. **If the 'agent'* is unknown (A), irrelevant (B), or self-evident (C)**
   * — the one who performs an action on the 'object'
   Example: *My wallet was stolen.*

Here, I want to say that I no longer have my wallet but (A) I don't know who stole it, or (B) this doesn't interest me or at least I'm not interested in guessing who did it, or (C) it's clear who did it — thieves! What more is there to say about that?

The same message in the Active Voice would be: *Someone stole my wallet.* Here, I'm avoiding any attempt to identify the agent.

3. **We want to avoid responsibility**. (We are hiding the fact that it's our fault or trying to soften the message).
   For example: *You'll be fired.* (I don't want to directly say that I'm a decision-maker here.)

The more sincere way to say it would be: *I'll get you fired,* or *I'll fire you.*

A definition of the Passive Voice from *Urbandictionary.com:* "*An ingenious grammatical feature that allows for one to completely disassociate oneself from an action, or to obliquely insult or soften the impact of a slight.*"

Active vs. Passive Voice

According to some research, everyday English speech consists of 97.5% Active Voice sentences. Scientific and journalistic texts consist of 82.2%.

So, this is our chart for the Passive Voice:

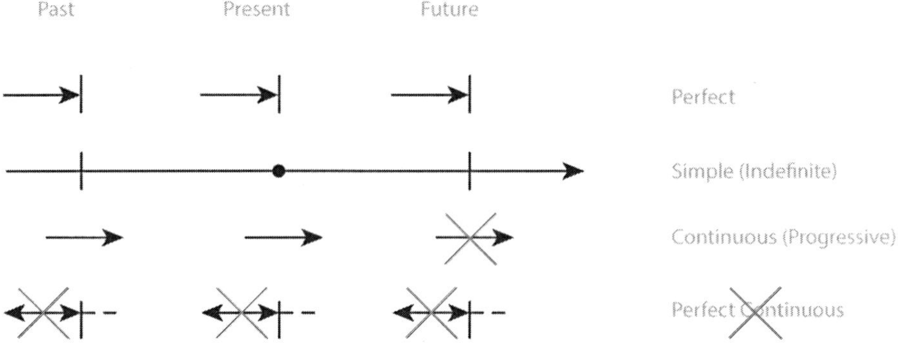

Actually, this one…

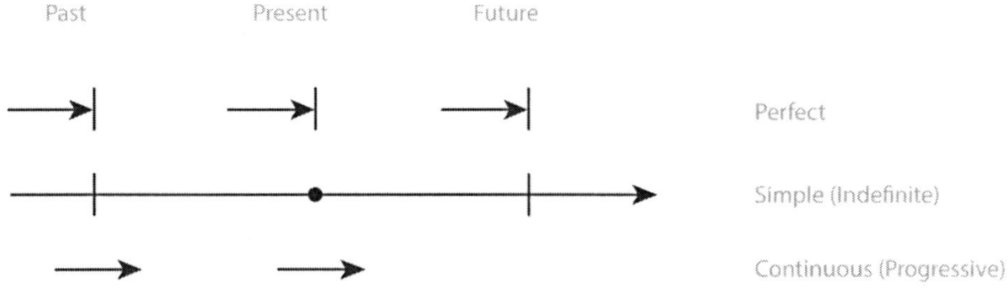

Passive voice – Formula

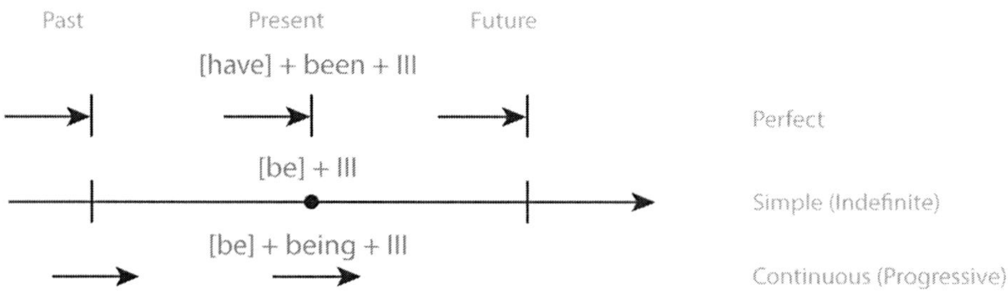

it had been installed ← it has been installed → it will have been installed

it was installed ← it is installed → it will be installed

it was being installed ← it is being installed → [no Future Continuous in Passive Voice]

The examples I use to memorize it:

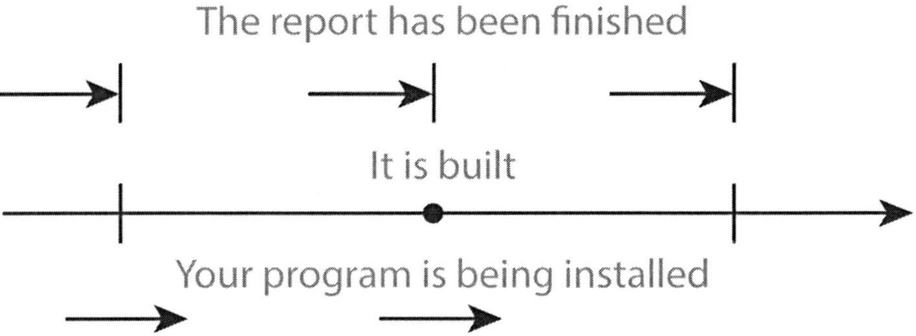

!   Try to think of your own examples, something you can relate to and easily
remember.

Practicing with different verbs

When practicing with different verbs, you may notice that not all verbs sound 'normal' in all tenses. For example, the verb *make* sounds okay in any tense both in the Active and the Passive Voice (i.e. in all twenty tenses).

The verb *buy* sounds a bit weird in some tenses. Phrases like, "*I will have been buying*" and "*it was being bought*" sound unnatural. Or you would need a very solid context before they start sounding natural.

But for the verb *like,* even a widespread tense as the Present Continuous sounds super weird. You get a clumsy grammatical construct sometimes called the '*Big Mac™ Progressive*'.*

But all this should not stop you from practicing. Take any verb (regular or irregular) and run it through all the tenses, just for practice. Forget about the meaning — this is a different exercise.

!   * — From the McDonald's ad campaign of 2003 — "*I'm lovin' it.*"
It was grammatically incorrect but catchy, hence super effective.
[*–in'* is the same as *–ing,* but the apostrophe signifies a nonchalant pronunciation and the '*g*' being silent]

Let's try to run the verb 'install' through the Chart

	Past	Present	Future	
	the program had been installed	*the program has been installed*	*the program will have been installed*	Perfect
	the program was installed	*the program is installed*	*the program will be installed*	Simple
	the program was being installed	*the program is being installed*		Continuous

Question — Moving the Auxiliary Verb* to the Beginning of the Sentence

* — Always only one word

	Past	Present	Future	
	had the program had been installed?	*has the program has been installed?*	*will the program will have been installed?*	Perfect
	was the program was installed?	*is the program is installed?*	*will the program will be installed?*	Simple
	was the program was being installed?	*is the program is being installed?*		Continuous

Negative — Putting Not After an Auxiliary* Verb

* — Sometimes after the linking verb [*be*], sometimes after a modal verb (*will*, *can*).

Past	Present	Future	
the program hadn't been installed	the program hasn't been installed	the program won't have been installed	Perfect
the program wasn't installed	the program isn't installed	the program won't be installed	Simple
the program wasn't being installed	the program isn't being installed		Continuous

Question — Through a Question Word

Question Words

- What?
- When?
- Where?
- Why?
- Which?
- Whose?
- Whom?
- How?

The Word Order Is the Same as Before, But Now You Put a Question Word at the Very Front of the Sentence

you go → you do go → you do not go → do you go? → where do you go?

auxiliary verb

Where do you go?

question word   subject   main verb

Question word + auxiliary verb + subject + main verb

You are going
Question: *Are you going?* (an auxiliary verb moved to the front of the sentence)
Adding a question word — *Where are you going?*

He eats (or: *He does eat*)
Question: *Does he eat?* (moved an auxiliary verb in front of the sentence)
Adding a question word — *What does he eat?*

They did that (or: *They did do that*)
Question: *Did they do that?* (moved an auxiliary verb in front of the sentence)
Adding a question word — *How did they do that?*

Reported (Indirect) Speech

There are many cases when we need to describe an event or action that happened — very often, that includes repeating what someone said. There are two types of speech used to describe what someone said: Direct Speech and Indirect Speech (or Reported Speech).

We use Direct Speech when we are simply repeating what someone says, word for word.

Example: *"I like ice cream," she said.*

When we want to report what someone said without necessarily using exactly the same words, we can use Indirect Speech.

Example: *She said that she liked ice cream.*

Indirect Speech

You need to note one thing about Indirect Speech…

Direct Speech — *"I like ice cream," she said.*
Indirect Speech — *She said that she liked ice cream.*

Have you noticed that *like* (Present Tense) in Direct Speech turned into *liked* (Past Tense) in Indirect Speech? The tense changes in reported speech.

This happened because when she was speaking, her love for ice cream was a fact, but at the moment when we are retelling the story, this information may be outdated. She may no longer love ice cream.

Indirect Speech

In Direct Speech, a verb can be used in any tense (in both the Active and Passive Voice). So, to memorize how tenses change, we'll use a visual key.

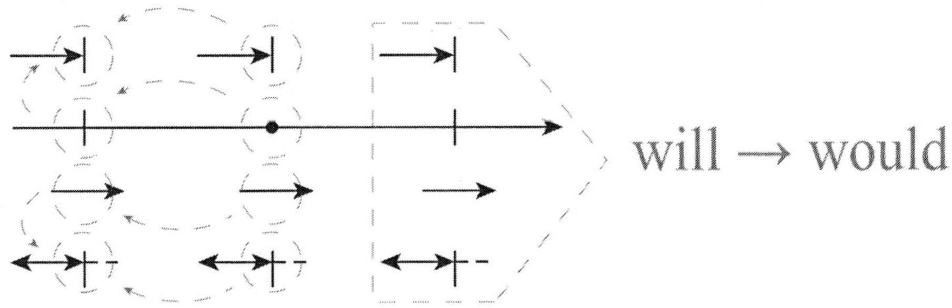

How to memorize the tense change in Indirect Speech sentences:

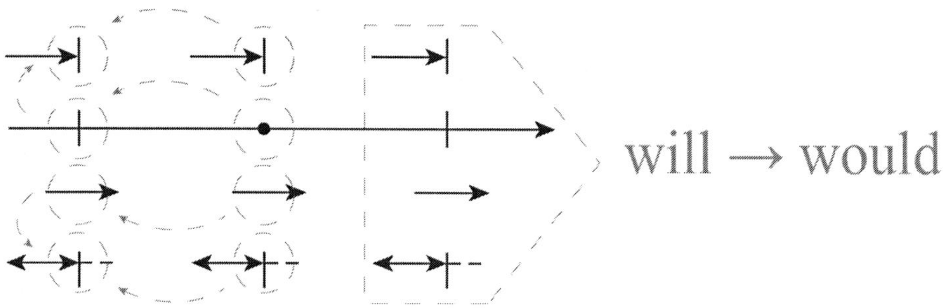

Direct Speech	Indirect Speech
He said: "My mother is here."	*He said that his mother was there.*

Indirect Speech — 'Tense Shift'

In all tense groups, you'll shift or slide back to the past:

1. Present Perfect → Past Perfect
2. Present Simple → Past Simple
3. Present Continuous → Past Continuous
4. Present Perfect Continuous → Past Perfect Continuous

Examples:

1. *I haven't seen... → She said that she hadn't seen...*
2. *I can speak... → She said she could speak...*
3. *I am living in London → She said (that) she was living in London*
4. *I have been waiting... → She said she had been waiting...*

Indirect Speech — 'Tense Shift' (Past)

1. Past Perfect – **stays the same** (Past Perfect)
2. Past Simple → Past Perfect
3. Past Continuous → Past Perfect Continuous
4. Past Perfect Continuous – **stays the same** (Past Perfect Continuous)

Examples:

1. *I had taken... → He said (that) he had taken...*
2. *I bought... → He said that he had bought...*
3. *I was walking → He said (that) he had been walking...*
4. *I had been waiting... → He said he had been waiting...*

Indirect Speech: Will → Would

The 'time shift' for future tenses means switching from *will* to *would*:

Direct Speech — *"I'll see you later," he said.*
Indirect Speech — *He said that he would see me later.*

Also: *can — could; may — might; must (have to) — had to; should — should* (not changing)

Indirect Speech: Active Voice

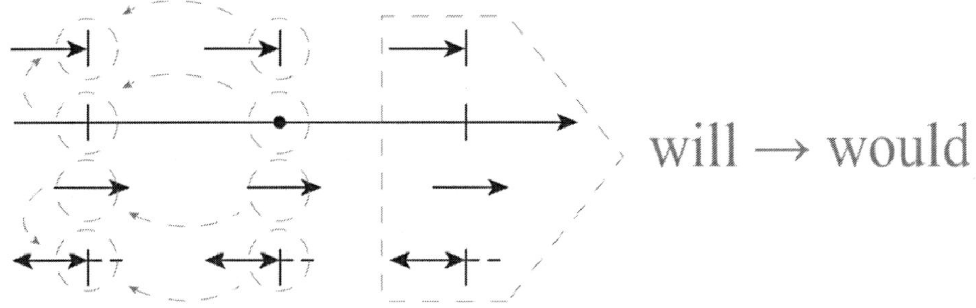

Indirect Speech — One more thing…

Some pronouns and adverbs will change accordingly:

Direct Speech	Indirect Speech
this, these	*that, those*
here	*there*
now	*then*
today	*that day*
tomorrow	*the next day*
yesterday	*the day before*

Indirect Speech: If it was a question…

If the Direct Speech was a question, in Indirect Speech, the question disappears, and the sentence turns into a dependent clause.

We can use *if* or *whether* to report indirect yes-no questions.

Direct Speech	Indirect Speech
He asked me, "Do you speak Spanish?"	*He asked me if (whether) I spoke Spanish.*

Direct speech questions asking 'who', 'what', 'when', 'where', 'why', and 'how' can be rephrased in Indirect Speech format. Question marks are not used in Indirect Speech formats.

Direct Speech	Indirect Speech
He asked me, "What is your name?"	*He asked me what my name was.*

Indirect Speech: Passive Voice

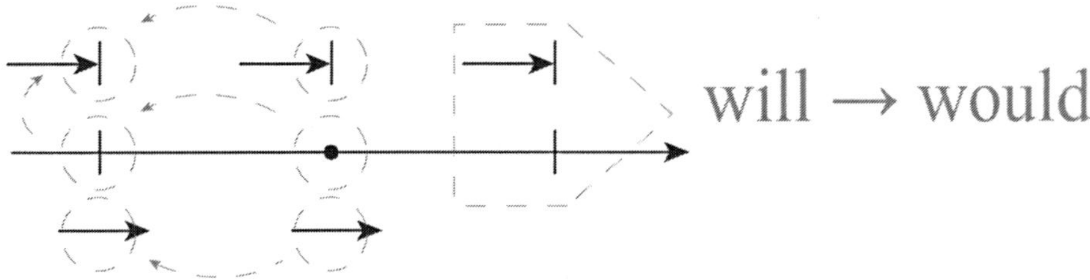

The same rule about tense-shifting applies to the Passive Voice. The present becomes the past:

1. Present Perfect → Past Perfect
2. Present Simple → Past Simple
3. Present Continuous → Past Continuous

Examples:

1. *I said: "A letter has been written..." → I said that a letter had been written...*
2. *I said: "A letter is written..." → I said that a letter was written...*
3. *I said: "A letter is being written..." → I said that a letter was being written...*

Indirect Speech: Passive Voice (Past)

Past:

1. Past Perfect — **stays the same** (Past Perfect)
2. Past Simple → Past Perfect
3. Past Continuous — **stays the same** (Past Continuous)

Examples:

1. *I said: "A letter had been written…" → I said that a letter had been written…*
2. *I said: "A letter was written…" → I said that a letter had been written…*
3. *I said: "A letter was being written…" → I said that a letter was being written…*

Indirect Speech: Passive Voice

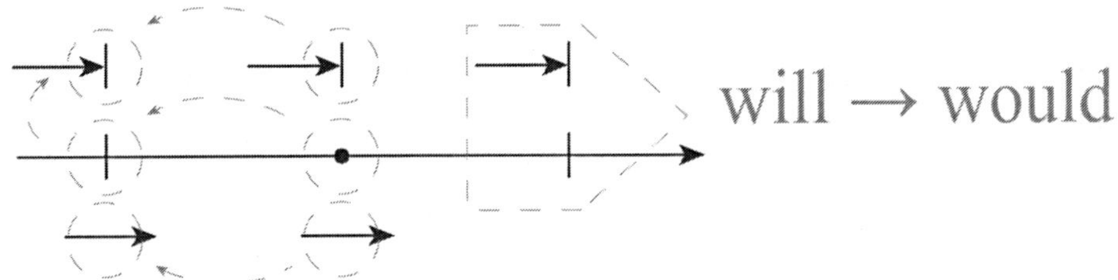

will → would; can → could; may → might; must (have to) → had to; should → should (does not change)

Direct Speech	Indirect Speech
I said: "A letter will be written."	*I said that a letter would be written.*

Future in the Past

We use the Future in the Past tense when we want to say that, in the past, we thought something would happen in the future. It does not matter if we were correct or not. The Future in the Past follows the same basic rules as the Simple Future. '*Would*' is used for volunteer actions or promises; '*was going to*' is used for plans. Both forms can be used to make predictions about the future.

Examples:

I told you he was going to come to the party. (plan)
I knew Julie would make dinner. (voluntary action)
Jane said Sam was going to bring his sister with him, but he came alone. (plan)
I had a feeling that the vacation was going to be a disaster. (prediction)
He promised he would send a postcard from Egypt. (promise)

Future in the Past: How is it formed?

the whole sentence

— *I thought the train would arrive on time*

main clause
Past Simple — *I thought…*

dependent clause
…what exactly did I think back than

The dependent clause is formed from one of the Future tenses (Future Perfect, Future Simple, Future Continuous, Future Perfect Continuous) by changing *will* to *would* (or in old texts *shall* to *should*). Main and dependent clauses can change places.

Future in the Past: Active Voice

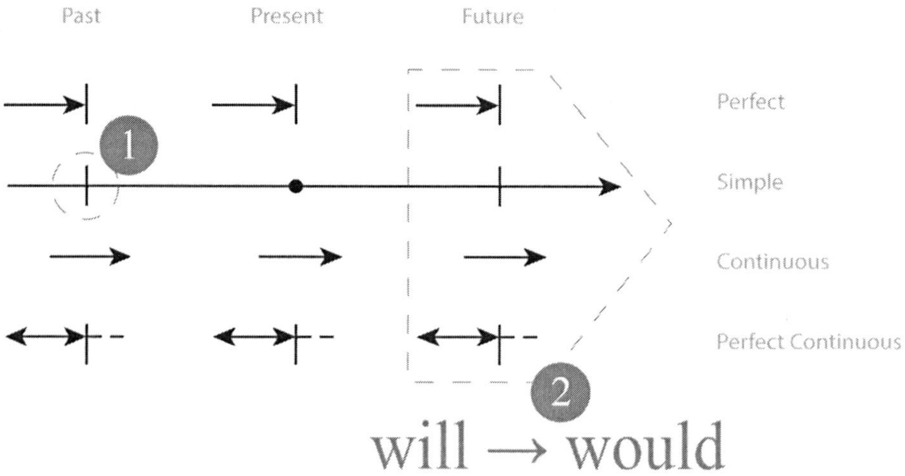

1. Main clause — in Past Simple
2. Dependent clause — formed with one of the four Future tenses by changing *will* to *would*.

Future in the Past: Active Voice

Tense	Example
Future Perfect in the Past	*He said he would have read the book by the time I needed it.*
Future Simple in the Past	*I thought that he would be late.*
Future Continuous in the Past	*I knew we would be packing next Friday*
Future Perfect Continuous in the Past	*He said that by that time he would have been driving for three hours*

Negative: To form the negative, simply add *not* after *would*.

I knew we would not be packing next Friday. (I knew we wouldn't be packing next Friday.)

Future in the Past: Passive Voice

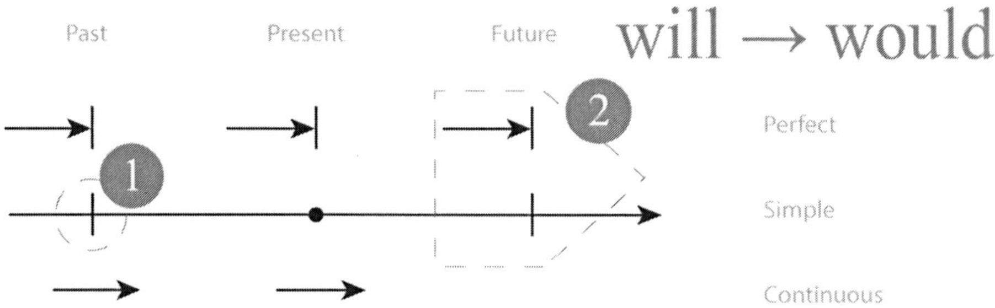

1. Main Clause — in Past Simple
2. Dependent clause — formed with one of two Future tenses by changing *will* to *would*.

Tense	Example
Future Perfect in the Past	*He knew the work would have been finished by Friday.*
Future Simple in the Past	*I thought the glass would be broken.*

Grammatical Forms

Speaking about the Future

The easiest way to talk about the Future is: *[be] + going to + verb**

> !   * Do not confuse it with: *[be] + going to + noun*
> This would be a Present Continuous with a main verb *go*. Example: *I'm going to school.*

[be] + going to + verb

I'm   *planning to*   *do*

Examples	...with [be] in the Past to get Future in the Past
I'm going to go.	*They were going to get married.*
He's not gonna do.	*Was she going to come?*

going to = gonna**

** — in spoken English

Speaking about the Past: used to + verb

The form *used to + verb* is used to describe an activity or state that happened many times in the past and is no longer true.

— *I used to smoke.* (I do not smoke anymore.)
— *He used to gamble when he was younger.* (He stopped gambling after he grew up.)
— *You used to be smarter.* (You started using social media more, and now you're not as smart.)
— *There used to be a farm there.* (Now, there is no farm there.)

The negative form in everyday speech is not typical, but possible nevertheless:

- *I didn't use to learn French.*

You add an extra *do* verb and apply the '*I-did-it-just-once*' rule... + add *not*.

I used to learn... → I did use to learn... → I didn't use to learn

Ask question by moving the auxiliary verb to the beginning of a sentence:

- *Did he use to do sports?*

He used to do sports. → He did use to do sports. → Did he use to do sports?

Do not confuse 'use' with 'used to + verb'

use	used to + verb
To use something	An activity that happened many times in the past but is not happening anymore.
I use subway every day.	*I used to like this movie but now I don't.*

[be] + used to + noun or gerund	[get] + used to + noun or gerund
Accustomed to something	Getting accustomed to something
She's (she is) used to getting up early.	*It's hard to get used to it…*
He was used to this climate.	*I'm getting used to driving on the left.*

Speaking of the past: would

Would is a verb that is used widely.

As an auxiliary verb, it is used to form the Future in the Past tense (*He told us he would come*) and express a conditional mood (*I wish they would come and visit us*).

As a modal verb, it expresses persistence, probability, or a kind request (*would you please...*).

But there is one more use for it:

Just like the form *used to* + *verb*, an auxiliary verb *would* describe things that happened many times in the past.

Example: *We would play with him every day* (when we were kids).

I would say…

…that apart from what's been mentioned regarding the use of the word *would*, namely:

1) Reported Speech
— *He said that he would see me later.*

2) Future in the Past
— *I knew he would do that.*

3) Nostalgic description of the Past
— *We would play with him every day.*

…in other cases, *would* can be used to talk about a possible or imagined situation or event.

— *I would buy this book. Wouldn't you?*

Conditionals

We have already touched on the use of the word would. So, why wouldn't we also mention the conditionals?

Conditionals describe the result of something that might happen (in the present or future) or might have happened but didn't (in the past).

Our Chart also helps us visualize which tenses are used when dealing with Conditionals. This is a topic many students struggle with for years, and a visual aid might help.

There are several structures in English that we call *Conditionals* or *If Conditionals*. The word 'condition' means 'situation or circumstance'. If a particular condition is true, then a particular result happens. We can also invert the two parts of a conditional sentence so that 'if' part comes second.

You can change the order of the 'if' clause and the main clause.

— If you finish your borsch, you'll have the cake.
— You'll have the cake if you finish your borsch first.

Conditionals

complex sentence

— *If you finish your borsch, you'll have the cake*

If clause
condition

Main clause
result

For different conditional sentences, both parts change grammatically.
It may be helpful to have a visual key again.

Zero Conditional

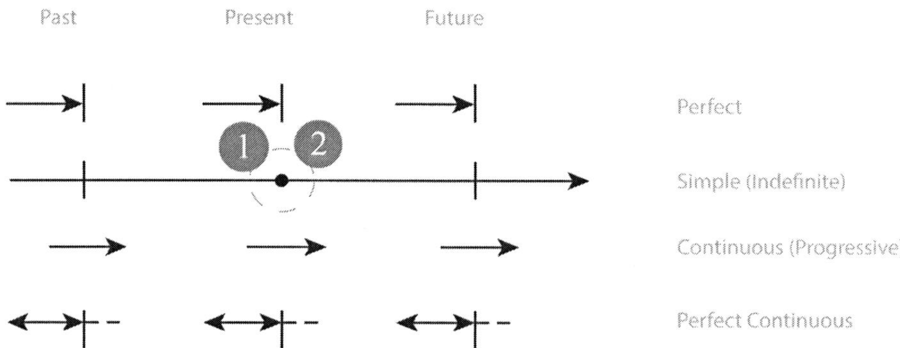

For the Zero Conditional, both the *if clause* (1) and the *main clause* (2) will be in the Present Simple.

— *If she needs money, I just give it to her.*

First Conditional

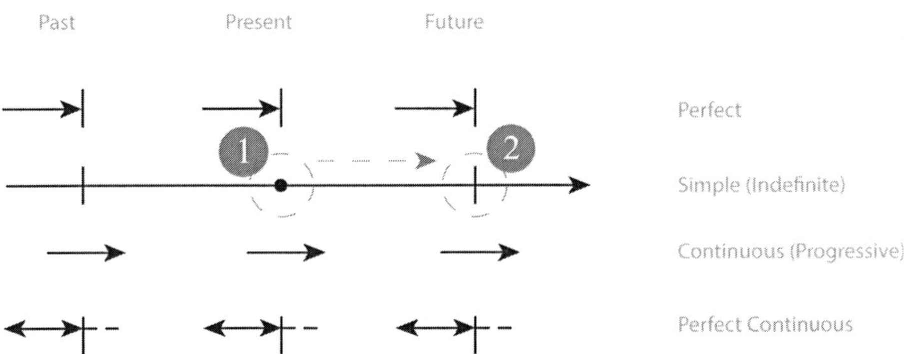

For the First Conditional, the if clause (1) is in the Present Simple, and the main clause (2) is in the Future Simple.

— *If she needs money, I will give it to her.*

Second Conditional

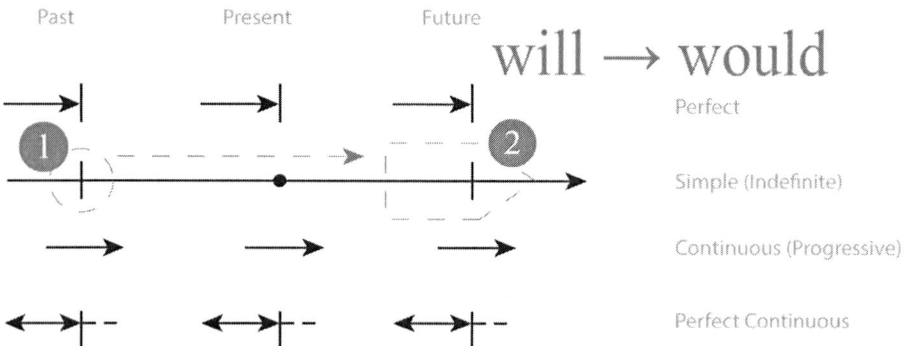

For the Second Conditional, the if clause (1) is in the Past Simple. The main clause (2) — is formed like Future Simple but *"will"* is replaced with *"would"* (just like for Indirect Speech or Future in the Past).

— *If she needed money, I would give it to her.*

Third Conditional

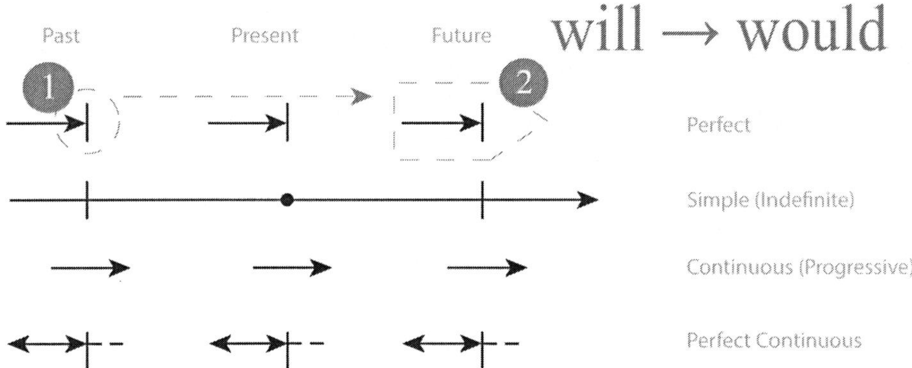

For the Third Conditional, the *if clause* (1) is in the Past Perfect. The *main clause (2) — is formed like* Future Perfect *but "will" is replaced with "would"*

— If she'd needed money, I would have just given it to her.

Conditionals

Type	Probability	Examples
0	fact	*If she needs money, I just give it to her.*
1	maybe	*If she needs money, I will give it to her.*
2	unlikely	*If she needed money, I would give it to her.*
3	it's too late	*If she'd needed money, I would have just given it to her.*

Mixed Conditionals

Mixed conditionals are exactly what they sound like — a conditional sentence that mixes two different times in one sentence.

Past Action → Present Result

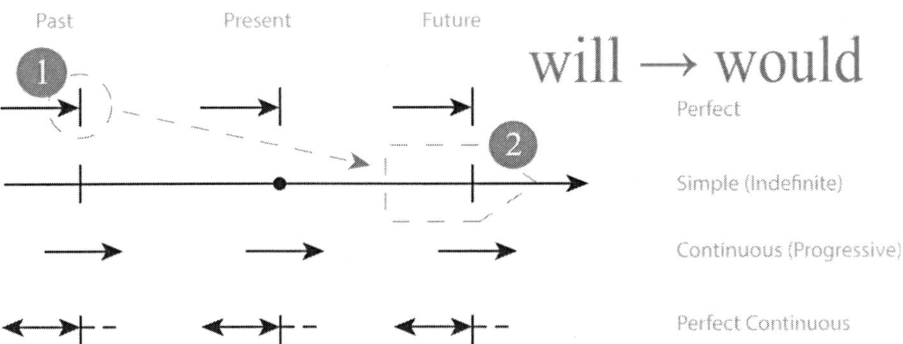

— *If I hadn't been so stingy, she would marry me.*

Mixed Conditionals

Present Condition → Past Result

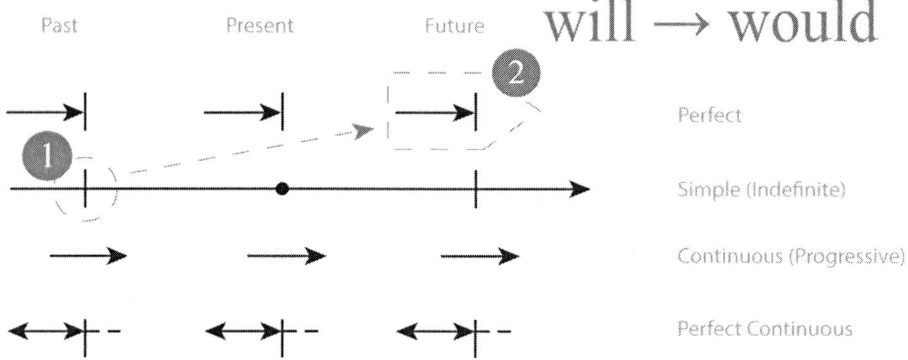

— *If she weren't such a bitch, I would have given her the money.*

Practice Exercise

Read each phrase and try to guess the tense.

I have been there

auxiliary verb   main verb

I have been there

I visited this place before

> **Present Perfect, Active Voice**
> Indication: *have* + *III* (of verb *be*)

it is changed (*it's changed*)

auxiliary verb [be]   main verb

it is changed (it's changed)
someone changes it all the time

Present Simple, Passive Voice
Indication: *[be] + III*

it has changed (it's changed)

auxiliary verb   main verb

it has changed *(it's changed)*

it changed itself or the result is

that it is changed now

Present Perfect, Active Voice
Indication: *[have] + III*

you have been living there

verb be in III form

auxiliary verb

main verb

you have been living there

it's been a while

Present Perfect Continuous, Active Voice
Indication: *have + been + ing*

I won't be coming

auxiliary verb be;
in the Future: will be;
negative form: will not be → won't be

main verb

I won't be coming

I will not be there (spoken language)

Future Continuous, Active Voice
Indication: *will be + ing*

it was mentioned

auxiliary verb   main verb

it was mentioned

Past Simple, Passive Voice
Indication: *was ([be] in the Past) + III*

you are a jerk

linking verb be

you are a jerk

throughout you life

Present Simple, Active Voice

you are being a jerk

auxiliary verb be

main verb be in *–ing* form
IV form, present participle

you are being a jerk

in this situation or at this moment

Present Continuous, Active Voice
Indication: *[be] + ing*

they were being sold at a low price

auxiliary verb be in *–ing* form
IV form, present participle

auxiliary verb be

main verb in a III form

they were being sold at a low price

Past Continuous, Passive Voice
Indication: *[be] (in its Past form) + being + III*

Let's Close a Couple of
Very Common Gaps:

Modal verbs

In the Past and Future, they change this way:

could ← can → will be able to

might ← may → will be allowed to ...

had to ← have to (has to) → will have to

had to ← must → will have to

Don't use *to* after modal verbs.

> *You must ~~to~~ do this...*
> *I can ~~to~~ swim...*
> *You should ~~to~~ buy it...*
> *You may ~~to~~ go now...*

! *have to* (and *ought to*) are exceptions. They are also modal verbs, but they are phrasal modal verbs, so to stays.

Noun, verb, adjective

When analyzing a sentence, please note that the same word may belong to a different part of speech (noun, verb, adjective, etc.), depending on the context.

Don't blindly trust your knowledge. Always make sure to check the context.

Here are some examples of words that most of us translate automatically without much thought. However, sometimes they have different meanings or belong to different parts of speech.

Noun	Verb	Adjective
In the summer, we camped in the open.	*I'll open the door.*	*He looked through the open door.*
The food was served on long tables.	*A number of amendments were tabled by the opposition.*	*a table lamp*

What to Do Now?

Fake It till You Make It!

- Read and listen to more content in English. Mimic (copy) what you hear and read.
- Use the tenses and grammatical structures of the language you are learning — this is exactly how we learned our native language as kids. We used to copy what adults said and their intonation and then observe people's reactions to phrases we were mimicking. Start doing the same with English. This is the only way to master it. Use the technique used naturally by children.
- Most language learning is not done through reading grammar books. You need a good book as a first push, and later for some self-correction. Most of the work is done in the field…in the wild, so to speak. Read! Listen! Talk to other people (natives preferably). Analyze! Correct yourself! Repeat!

Correcting Yourself

- Do not try to be perfect in your speech and writing. You are risking putting yourself into a depression. Desiring to be perfect may prevent you from writing or saying anything at all. In the spirit of the Pareto Law, being 80% good is good enough. The main goal of language learning (usually) is to facilitate communication. Sometimes, it doesn't matter how many mistakes you've made; you did great if you were understood.

- But if you want to keep improving your grammar, make a habit of replaying in your mind each conversation you have had. Try to analyze and correct all the phrases that you and your conversation partner have used.

- Don't be satisfied with the basics! Of course, it all depends on the goals you have in your language acquisition, but it's always best to aim high. Just like swaying some dumbbells in the gym doesn't automatically make you fit, mediocre language skills are not going to bring you closer to your English-speaking friends, colleagues, or people you encounter on your trip abroad.

Neural Circuits

- Every time we say a word or phrase, we reinforce a specific neural circuit. The more we repeat it, the easier it becomes for the signal to select the most familiar pathway. The neural circuit gets stronger, and the skill becomes easier to repeat. And the brain gets lazy and complacent.
- Every time we use the wrong phrase or pronounce something incorrectly, we are cementing a wrong skill. We are risking having it wrong (on a biological level) for the rest of our lives.
- The brain is lazy. It doesn't want to bother creating new neural circuits. It wants to use the old ones. So, try to fight back.
- Be patient! As we grow older, we tend to expect instant results with no extra effort.
- Your goal is to write and pronounce everything *correctly* more times than incorrectly.

Don't Shift Responsibility onto Anyone Else

- Don't think that you've *'already done your part'* by taking English classes. Do not shift responsibility for your goals onto others.
- Think about how little children learn to speak their language. They listen and repeat. They make mistakes. But with time, correction by adults, and immersing themselves in the environment, they improve. Most of them, anyways…Start doing the same thing.
- It's like going to the gym — it's not your personal trainer who needs to lift weights for you to get fit. You need to do all the heavy lifting yourself!

How to Get English-Language Practice

These suggestions are nothing new, but they are good reminders:

- Find a pen pal (or strategically fall in love with a native speaker...).
- Watch your favorite TV series and movies again and again, paying attention to the phrasing and pronunciation.
- Read (and re-read) your favorite books in English.
- Always have a grammar book handy. Use it when you are in doubt (and it is convenient to do so).
- Use a good electronic dictionary. The best ones are:
1. Longman Dictionary of Contemporary English.
2. Cambridge Advanced Learners Dictionary.
3. Oxford Advanced Learner's Dictionary.
4. Merriam-Webster's Advanced Learner's Dictionary.

The Four Secrets of Learning a New Language

Mastering any language consists of four main skills:

1. Speaking
2. Listening
3. Reading
4. Writing

Well, then…

…there are also four secrets to language learning — all of which are well-known to polyglots:

1. Speak more!
2. Listen more!
3. Read more!
4. And write more!

The formula for success

time you spend studying

$$\text{talent} \times t = \text{result}$$

your personal aptitude
to a new language acquisition

! Even if you do not have a great talent for learning languages, you can still get excellent results if you focus on the second factor, which is…

…studying regularly. Yes, this is completely unoriginal advice but effective. Studying every day would be ideal, even if it's just for ten minutes. It's much better than twice a week for 1–2 hours, which is the pattern that most language schools recommend.

That is it!
Good luck!